ORAL LITERATURE IN THE DIGITAL AGE

World Oral Literature Series: Volume 2

Oral Literature in the Digital Age:
Archiving Orality and Connecting with Communities

Edited by

Mark Turin, Claire Wheeler and
Eleanor Wilkinson

OpenBook
Publishers

Open Book Publishers CIC Ltd.
40 Devonshire Road, Cambridge, England CB1 2BL
http://www.openbookpublishers.com

This is the second volume in the World Oral Literature Series, published in
association with the World Oral Literature Project.
ISSN: 2050-7933

As with all Open Book Publishers titles, digital material and resources associated
with this volume are available from our website at:
http://www.openbookpublishers.com/isbn/9781909254305

ISBN Hardback: 978-1-909254-31-2
ISBN Paperback: 978-1-909254-30-5
ISBN Digital (PDF): 978-1-909254-32-9
ISBN Digital ebook (epub): 978-1-909254-33-6
ISBN Digital ebook (mobi): 978-1-909254-34-3

DOI: 10.111647/OBP.0032

Cover image: A Pochury woman listens to a recording of her own singing. Kohima
(Nagaland), 2005. Photo: Alban von Stockhausen.

Typesetting by www.bookgenie.in

All paper used by Open Book Publishers is SFI (Sustainable Forestry Initiative), and
PEFC (Programme for the Endorsement of Forest Certification Schemes) Certified.

Printed in the United Kingdom and United States by
Lightning Source for Open Book Publishers

Contents

Editors

Mark Turin is a linguistic anthropologist specialised in the Himalayas. He directs the World Oral Literature Project and the Digital Himalaya Project, both of which are co-located at Cambridge and Yale universities. He is the author or co-author of four books, the editor of five volumes and has published numerous articles and book chapters. He is the Program Director of Yale's new Himalaya Initiative.

Claire Wheeler is a Research Assistant at the World Oral Literature Project. She has a background in Modern and Medieval Languages, educational publishing, and teaching English as a foreign language.

Eleanor Wilkinson is a Research Assistant at the World Oral Literature Project. She has a background in ancient languages and culture, and has previously worked as a freelance collections assistant after completing her MA in Museum Studies.

Contributors

Felix K. Ameka is a linguist who teaches in the African Languages and Cultures programme at Leiden University. His relevant research interests are in ethnography of communication, semantics, pragmatics, socio-historical linguistics and the reflexive relations between language, culture and cognition and West African languages especially Gbe and Ghana-Togo Mountain languages.

Judith Aston is a Senior Lecturer in Film-making and Creative Media at the University of the West of England in Bristol, holding a PhD in Computer-related Design from the Royal College of Art and a Master's degree in Social Science from the University of Cambridge. As a new media pioneer in the mid 1980s, she has extensive experience of working with digital archives, interactive documentary, and expanded film, through which she continues to develop her longstanding interests in sensory ethnography and cross-cultural communication.

Kofi Dorvlo is a Senior Research Fellow in the Language Centre, University of Ghana. He currently works on the documentation of the languages and cultures of the peoples of the Ghana Togo Mountain area. He is also a part-time lecturer at the University of Health and Allied Sciences, Ho in Ghana. He gained his undergraduate degree in English and Linguistics at Legon and did his graduate work in the same University. He was awarded a PhD in Linguistics at Leiden University, Netherlands.

Margaret Field is a Professor of American Indian Studies at San Diego State University. She received her PhD in Linguistics at the University of California Santa Barbara.

Paul Matthews is a Senior Lecturer in Information Science and Web Development at the University of the West of England. Paul's research interests include digital libraries, multimedia search and the dynamics of knowledge exchange on the social web.

Madan Meena is a practicing artist with an education in Fine Arts. His interest in folk culture studies motivated him to gradually become a folklorist.

Daniela Merolla lectures African Literatures at the Department of African Languages and Cultures, Centre for the Arts in Society, University of Leiden, The Netherlands. Her research focuses on African oral literary productions (Tamazight, Algeria/Morocco, and Ewe, Ghana) as well as on written literatures in African and European languages. She published among others: "Digital Imagination and the 'Landscapes of Group Identities': Berber Diaspora and the Flourishing of Theatre, Videos, and Amazigh-Net", The Journal of North African Studies, 2002, pp. 122–131; "Dangerous Love in mythical narratives and formula tales", Religion, vol.39, 2009, pp. 283–288; and edited (with E. Bekers and S. Helff) "Transcultural Modernities: Narrating Africa in Europe", Amsterdam: Rodopi, 2009; and (with J. Jansen and K. Naït-Zerrad) "Multimedia Research and Documentation of Oral Genres in Africa—The Step Forward", Köln: Köppe Verlag, 2012.

Mingzhu Ha was born in 1989 in Hawan Village, Tiantang Town, Tianzhu Tibetan Autonomous County, Gansu Province, China. Like her elder brother, Mingzong, she studied English at Qinghai Normal University. Currently she is working on her BA in Environmental Science at Asian University for Women in Bangladesh.

Mingzong Ha was born in 1987 in Hawan Village, Tiantang Town, Tianzhu Tibetan Autonomous County, Gansu Province, China. He studied English/ Tibetan at Qinghai Normal University (China) from 2002 to 2005, and Mongolian/Czech at Charles University in Prague (Czech Republic) from 2006 to 2012. Currently he is pursuing his second master's degree in management at the University of Cambridge.

David Nathan is the Director of the Endangered Languages Archive (ELAR) at SOAS, University of London, where he and his team have developed new approaches to the archiving of endangered languages resources. David has 20 years' experience in educational and computing support for endangered languages, through teaching, training, academic publishing, and developing multimedia for language learning and revitalisation. He is interested in the connections between language documentation, language support and linguistic research, and how these connections can be supported through innovative media technologies.

Jorge Gómez Rendón (1971) is an Ecuadorian linguist and anthropologist. His work focuses on documentation of endangered languages as well as on linguistic and cultural rights of indigenous peoples in Ecuador.

C. K. Stuart has lived in Inner Mongolia Autonomous Region, Qinghai Province, and Xi'an City, PR China; Ulaanbaatar, Mongolia; and Dumaguete, Negros Oriental since 1984. A native of Albion, Pushmataha County, Oklahoma, he currently teaches English, writes, and edits at Shaanxi Normal University.

Thomas Widlok (PhD in anthropology, LSE 1994) has carried out long-term field research in Namibia over more than three decades. He is currently professor of anthropology at Radboud University Nijmegen and will take up a chair at the University of Cologne in 2013.

Introduction

Mark Turin, Claire Wheeler and Eleanor Wilkinson

Collecting, protecting and connecting oral literature

This volume is an essential guide and handbook for ethnographers, field linguists, community activists, curators, archivists, librarians, and all who connect with indigenous communities in order to document and preserve oral traditions.

For societies in which traditions are conveyed more through speech than through writing, oral literature has long been the mode of communication for spreading ideas, knowledge and history. The term "oral literature" broadly includes ritual texts, curative chants, epic poems, folk tales, creation stories, songs, myths, spells, legends, proverbs, riddles, tongue-twisters, recitations and historical narratives. In most cases, such traditions are not translated when a community shifts to using a more dominant language.

Oral literatures are in decline as a result of a cultural focus on literacy, combined with the disappearance of minority languages. The *Atlas of the World's Languages in Danger*,[1] released by UNESCO in early 2009, claims that around a third of the 6,500 languages spoken around the globe today are in danger of disappearing forever. Globalisation and rapid socio-economic change exert particularly complex pressures on smaller communities of speakers, often eroding expressive diversity and transforming culture through assimilation to more dominant ways of life. Until relatively recently, few indigenous peoples have had easy access to effective tools to document

1   See <http://www.unesco.org/culture/languages-atlas/> [Accessed 19 November 2012].
DOI: 10.111647/OBP.0032.01

their own cultural knowledge, and there is still little agreement on how collections of oral literature should be responsibly managed, archived and curated for the future.

The online archiving of audio and video recordings of oral literature is a technique of cultural preservation that has been widely welcomed by indigenous communities around the world. The World Oral Literature Project, established at the University of Cambridge in 2009 and co-located at Yale University since 2011, has a mission to "collect, protect and connect" endangered traditions. The Project facilitates partnerships between fieldworkers, archivists, performers of oral literature, and community representatives to document oral literature in ways that are ethically and practically appropriate. Our fieldwork grant scheme has funded the collection of audio and video recordings from nine countries in four continents. In addition, Project staff have digitised and archived older collections of oral literature, as well as contemporary recordings that are "born digital" but which were funded by other sources. At present, these collections represent a further twelve countries, amounting to over 400 hours of audio and video recordings of oral traditions now hosted for free on secure servers on the Project website.[2]

The World Oral Literature Project's strong focus on cooperation and understanding ensures that source communities retain full copyright and intellectual property over recordings of their traditions. Materials are protected for future posterity through accession to a secure digital archival platform with a commitment to migrating files to future digital formats as new standards emerge. Returning digitised materials to performers and communities frequently helps to protect established living traditions, with materials used for language education as well as programmes that aim to revitalise cultural heritage practices.[3] The inclusion of extensive metadata, including contextual details relating to the specific oral literature performance alongside its history and cultural significance, allows researchers and interested parties from diverse disciplines to connect with and experience the performative power of the collection. For example, while a musicologist might study the instrumental technique of a traditional song, a linguist would focus on grammatical structures in the verse, and an anthropologist might explore the social meaning and

---

2   See <http://www.oralliterature.org/collections> [Accessed 19 November 2012].
3   See the Digital Return research network for more discussion on these issues: <http://digitalreturn.wsu.edu> [Accessed 19 November 2012].

cultural values conveyed through the lyrics. Innovative digital archiving techniques support the retrieval of granular metadata that is relevant to specific research interests, alongside providing an easy way to stream or download the audio and video files from the web. In this manner, we have been able to connect recordings of oral literature to a broad community of users and researchers. In turn, this contributes to an appreciation of the beauty and complexity of human cultural diversity.

Coming together, sharing practices

The second annual workshop hosted by the World Oral Literature Project at the University of Cambridge in 2010, entitled *Archiving Orality and Connecting with Communities*, brought together more than 60 ethnographers, field linguists, community activists, curators, archivists and librarians. Organised with support from the Centre for Research in the Arts, Social Sciences and Humanities (CRASSH), Cambridge; the Department of Social Anthropology at the University of Cambridge; and the Netherlands Organisation for Scientific Research (NWO), the assembled delegates explored key issues around the dissemination of oral literature through traditional and digital media. Presentations from representatives of institutions in eight countries prompted fieldworkers to consider how best to store and disseminate their recordings and metadata; while archivists and curators were exposed to new methods of managing collections with greater levels of cultural sensitivity and through cooperative partnerships with cultural stakeholders.

Workshop panels were focused around a central theme: When new publics consume, manipulate and connect with field recordings and digital archival repositories of linguistic and cultural content, their involvement raises important practical and ethical questions about access, ownership, and permanence. These issues are reflected in a current trend among funding agencies, including the World Oral Literature Project's own fieldwork grants programme, to encourage fieldworkers to return copies of their material to source communities, as well as to deposit collections in institutional repositories. Thanks to ever-greater digital connectivity, wider Internet access and affordable multimedia recording technologies, the locus of dissemination and engagement has grown beyond that of researcher and research subject to include a diverse constituency of global users such as migrant workers, indigenous scholars, policymakers and journalists, to name but a few. Participants at the workshop explored key issues around the dissemination of oral literature, reflecting particularly on the impact of greater digital connectivity in extending the dissemination of fieldworkers' research and collections beyond traditional audiences.

Emerging from some of the most compelling presentations at the workshop, chapters in Part 1 of this volume raise important questions about the political repercussions of studying marginalised languages; the role of online tools in ensuring responsible access to sensitive cultural materials; and methods of avoiding fossilisation in the creation of digital documents. Part 2 consists of workshop papers presented by fieldworkers in anthropology and linguistics, all of whom reflect on the processes and outcomes of their own fieldwork and its broader relevance to their respective disciplines.

In keeping with our mandate to widen access and explore new modes of disseminating resources and ideas, workshop presentations are now available for online streaming and download through the World Oral Literature Project website.[4] Many of the chapters in this edited volume discuss audio and video recordings of oral traditions. Since a number of contributors have made use of online resources to illustrate their discussions on cultural property and traditional knowledge, it is hoped that readers will interact with this freely available media. URL links for referenced resources are included in a list of Online Sources in the reference section at the end of each chapter. All web resources were active at the time of publication unless otherwise stated.

Part I. Principles and Methods of Archiving and Conservation

Thomas Widlok's chapter discusses two aspects of digital archiving: first, he analyses what is actually involved in the process of digitisation and electronic archiving of spoken language documentation; second, he discusses notions of access and property rights in relation to the digital archives that result from such documentation. His emphasis in both cases is on identifying the elements and layers that make up the complex whole of the archive, yet he is quick to point out that there is more to this whole than is covered by his analysis. While Widlok's evaluation is based on

---

4   See <http://www.oralliterature.org/research/workshops.html> [Accessed 19 November 2012].

personal experience rather than a sample of projects, he acknowledges that themes of access and property rights in digitisation remain a recurring concern. The concluding argument of his chapter is that by viewing the component parts of the process of digital archiving for just one case study, we can see some of the contradictions and ambivalences of this process in more general terms. Through such a structural analysis, we may also begin to understand the mixed feelings that some field researchers have with regard to electronic archiving and online databasing. Widlok proposes that breaking these complex processes down into their elements may help us to make informed decisions about the extent and type of digital archiving we want to engage in.

David Nathan continues with the theme of digital archiving by considering the issue of access in relation to archives that hold documents of, and documentation relating to, endangered languages. Nathan defines access as the means of finding a resource; the availability of the resource; the delivery of the resource to the user; the relevance and accessibility of resource content to the user; and the user's perceptions of their experience interacting with the archive and its resources. His discussion is centred around the Endangered Languages Archive (ELAR) and its online catalogue, both based at the School of Oriental and African Studies (SOAS), London. The system uses features that have been pioneered in Web 2.0 or social networking applications, and is innovative in applying such techniques to language archiving. Nathan illustrates how ELAR's access system represents a true departure from conventional archival practices in the field of language documentation.

Nathan explains how until recently, access has been thought of as "online resource discovery through querying standardised metadata" (page 23, this volume). Where access control has been applied, it has typically been based on a formal membership criterion, such as a user account on a university's network. ELAR's goal is to provide an archive that is more closely tied to the needs of those working with endangered languages, and, of course, the needs of members of speech communities. Nathan reports on how this has emerged as a rich area of exploration, and, coupled with the rise of social networking applications and conventions over the last five years, has yielded a system that highlights the nuanced dynamics of access.

Judith Aston and Paul Matthews discuss the outcomes of a collaborative project between the authors and the Oxford-based anthropologist Wendy James. The authors report on their work with James to convert a collection of recordings into an accessible and usable digital archive that has relevance for contemporary users. Aston and Matthews describe James' fieldwork recordings from the Blue Nile Region of the Sudan-Ethiopian borderlands, which consist of spoken memories, interviews, conversations, myths and songs. Most of the original recordings are in the Uduk language, but the collection also contains material in other minority tongues, as well as national languages. The authors highlight how this archive needs to be useful both to academics and to a wider general public, but also, and most particularly, to the people themselves who are now starting to document and recall their own experiences. It is also important that the materials contained within the archive are perceived to be part of a wider set of regional records from north-east Africa, linked to diaspora communities now living in various parts of the world.

A key issue that emerges from Aston and Matthews' collaboration with James is the need to remain true to the fluidity of oral tradition over time, in order to avoid fossilisation and misrepresentation. Their chapter recommends a conversational approach through which the archive can reveal the interactions and silences of informants, both in conversation with each other and with the ethnographer, at different historical periods. In developing such an approach, the authors hope that future users of the archive will be offered an opportunity to enter a sensory-rich world of experiences, one which foregrounds the awareness and agency of the people themselves and allows their voices to be heard in their vernacular language wherever possible.

Part II: Engagements and Reflections from the Field

Merolla, Ameka and Dorvlo open this volume's collection of field reports with a discussion of the scientific and ethical problems regarding the selection, authorship and audience that they encountered during a video-documentation research project on Ewe oral literature in south-eastern Ghana. Their documentation is based on an interview that Dorvlo and Merolla recorded in Accra in 2007. This interview concerns Ewe migration stories and is included in Merolla and Leiden University's Verba Africana series that includes videos of African oral genres with translations and interpretive commentaries informed by scientific research. The authors illustrate how the documentation and investigation of African oral genres is still largely based on materials provided in written form, although nowadays it is largely accepted that collecting and analysing printed transcriptions and translations only gives a faint portrait of oral poems and tales and their literary and social functions.

This chapter offers an insight into the difficulties of selecting video documentation on Ewe migration stories that is suitable to be presented to a broad audience of academics, students, a public interested in African oral genres, and those involved with cultural issues or invested in specific linguistic traditions. Merolla, Ameka and Dorvlo also enter into a larger debate that is active in all disciplines in which fieldwork is a central activity: the relationship between researchers and the researched, and the locus of responsibility for what is produced and published. The authors conclude by reflecting on the yet harder questions of ownership that arise when scholars make use of audio-visual media and when the final video document is available on the Internet. They offer elegant solutions by considering individual as well as collective indigenous peoples' rights, and advocate for stronger collaborations between researchers, performers and audience. The authors conclude by demonstrating how their own research strategies have resulted in culturally significant video documents that offer a contemporary snapshot of local knowledge.

Margaret Field's account focuses on the importance of American Indian oral literature for cultural identity and language revitalisation, demonstrated through the analysis of a trickster tale. Taking the position that oral literature such as narrative and song often serve as important cultural resources that retain and reinforce cultural values and group identity, Field demonstrates how American Indian trickster tales—like Aesop's fables found in Europe—contain moral content, and are typically aimed at child audiences. In this chapter, Field discusses an example of this genre with specific reference to the Kumeyaay community of Baja California, Mexico. She also describes how such stories are an important form of cultural property that index group identity: once through the code that is used, and then again through the content of the narrative itself. Field demonstrates how oral traditions such as trickster tales form an important body of knowledge that not only preserves cultural values and philosophical orientations, but also continues to instill these values in listeners.

Considering the uses of her own fieldwork, Field explains that American Indian communities typically view their oral traditions as communal intellectual property. It is therefore incumbent upon researchers who work with traditional texts in oral communities to collaborate to ensure that collected texts are treated in a manner that is appropriate from the perspective of the communities of origin. Field reminds us that it is essential for researchers to bear in mind the relationship between the recording, publication, and archiving of oral literature, community preferences regarding these aspects of research, and considerations relating to language revitalisation. Her message is particularly relevant today in light of the wide availability of multimedia and the ever-expanding capabilities for the archiving of oral literature. Through technological advancements, such recordings may be more available than ever in a range of formats (audio and video in addition to print), and ever more important (and political), as indigenous languages become increasingly endangered. Field concludes by demonstrating how her research materials were repatriated to the Kumayaay community in the form of educational resources and as reminders of cultural identity.

Jorge Gómez Rendón continues the discussion on revitalisation practices in the cultural heritage sector through his account of orality and literacy among indigenous cultures in Ecuador, paying close attention to contextual political factors and challenges. While Ecuador is the smallest of the Andean nations, it is linguistically highly diverse. Rendón explains that education programmes have not yet produced written forms of indigenous languages in Ecuador, which are now critically endangered. However, a resurgence of ethnic pride combined with increasing interest shown by governmental agencies in the safeguarding of cultural diversity are bringing native languages and oral practices to the foreground. This greater visibility is opening up new ways for linguistic identities to be politically managed.

After a review of the relative vitality of Ecuadorian indigenous languages and an evaluation of twenty years of intercultural bilingual education, Rendón focuses on two alternative approaches to orality in the fields of bilingual education and intangible cultural heritage. In discussing these two approaches, he addresses several ethical and legal issues concerning property rights, the dissemination of documentation outcomes, and the appropriation of intangible cultural heritage for the improvement of indigenous education. He provides a preliminary exploration into best practices in the archiving and management of digital materials for educational and cultural purposes in community contexts, through which Rendón proposes a "new model of intercultural bilingual education" and "safeguarding of intangible heritage [...] respecting [performers'] property rights from a collective rather than individual perspective" (page 79, this volume) with the aim of ensuring the survival of endangered languages and cultures.

Madan Meena's field report is based on his archiving experiences as a grantee of the World Oral Literature Project's fieldwork grants scheme. His focal recording was made in Thikarda village in south-eastern Rajasthan—a region locally known as Hadoti—and was performed in the Hadoti language in a distinct singing style. Geographically, the area is very large (24,923 square kilometers), and there are many variations in the style of performance. Meena offers an account of his experience recording the twenty-hour Hadoti ballad of Tejaji, describing the challenges he faced in capturing the entire ballad in a manner that was as authentic as possible. Meena reports how, in the past, the ballad could only be performed at a shrine in response to a snake bite. Increasingly, however, as the belief systems behind the ballad are being challenged by education and Western medical techniques of treating snake bites, the ballad is becoming divorced from its religious roots and evolving into a distinct musical tradition of its own that can be performed at festivals for entertainment value. Meena describes the use of the project's resultant digital recordings by community members to popularise their traditional performances, using MP3 players and mobile phone handsets to listen to recordings. He reflects on the invaluable nature of digital technology in preserving oral cultures, alongside the threats posed by these same technological developments to more traditional performance of oral traditions.

In the final field report of this volume, Ha Mingzong, Ha Mingzhu and Charles K. Stuart describe their research on the Mongghul (Monguor, Tu) Ha Clan oral history tradition in Qinghai and Gansu provinces, China. The authors provide historical details on the Mongghul ethnic group, and justify the urgency of their fieldwork to record and preserve the cultural heritage and historical knowledge of Mongghul elders. As well as knowing a rich repertoire of songs, folktales and cultural expressions, these elders are the "last group able to repeat generationally transmitted knowledge about clan origins, migration routes, settlement areas, important local figures, [...] clan genealogy, [...], modes of livelihood, [and] relationships local people had with government" (page 94, this volume). Recognition is given to the importance of documenting such knowledge for the future benefit of younger generations.

Mingzong, Mingzhu and Stuart describe their method of recording interviews about family stories told by community members. Local reactions to their recording methods are explained, with the assurance that the fieldworkers were met with hospitality and a shared sense of the importance of the documentation from older community members, despite an initially indifferent attitude from younger members of the community. The authors provide examples of their transcriptions of interviews and demonstrate how the return of digital versions of the recordings to the community has strengthened the sense of clan unity and belonging.

Openness, access and connectivity

As editors of this volume, we are delighted to bring together these important contributions that reflect on the ethical practices of anthropological and linguistic fieldwork, digital archiving, and the repatriation of cultural materials. We believe that the widest possible dissemination of such work will help support the propagation of best practices to all who work in these fields. The open access publishing model practiced by our partners in this series, the Cambridge-based Open Book Publishers, is designed to ensure that these chapters are widely and freely accessible for years to come, on a range of different publishing platforms.

Open Book Publishers are experimental and innovative, changing the nature of the traditional academic book: publishing in hardback, paperback, PDF and e-book editions, but also offering a free online edition that can be read via their website.[5] Their commitment to open access dovetails with our Project's mandate to widen the dissemination of knowledge, ideas, and access to cultural traditions. Connecting with a broader audience—one that was historically disenfranchised by the exclusivity of print and the restrictive distribution networks that favoured Western readers—allows the protection of cultural knowledge. This is achieved through a better understanding of human diversity, and the return of digitised collections to source communities and countries of origin. The chapters in this volume help us to understand each stage of this journey, from building cooperative relationships with community representatives in the field, designing and using digital tools for cultural documentation, through to the ethical and

---

5   See <http://www.openbookpublishers.com/> [Accessed 22 April 2013].

practical considerations involved in building access models for digital archives.

When Edward Morgan Forster ended his 1910 novel *Howards End* with the powerful epigraph "Only connect..." he could not have imagined how this exhortation would resonate with generations to come and how its meaning would change.[6] For our purposes, both in this edited collection and in our work more generally in the World Oral Literature Project, "only connect" has a powerful, double meaning. First, and perhaps overwhelmingly for young audiences and readers, it implies that one is on the path to being digitally hooked up, wired (although in an increasingly wireless world, even the term "wired" is antiquated), and ready to participate in a virtual, online conversation. Since most of our transactions and communications in the Project are digital—through email, websites, voice-over Internet Protocol, and file share applications—"only connect" reflects our fast changing world and new work practices. Second, and perhaps more profoundly, "only connect" is what we hope to achieve when we share recordings of oral literature in print, on air and online. Connectivity is all: our project would not exist without the technical underpinnings and the philosophical imperative to see information and knowledge shared. We hope that you enjoy reading this volume as much as we have enjoyed editing it and that you will, quite simply, connect.

Cambridge, November 2012

---

6   Published in London by Edward Arnold.

I. Principles and Methods of Archiving and Conservation

1. The Archive Strikes Back: Effects of Online Digital Language Archiving on Research Relations and Property Rights

Thomas Widlok

An analysis of research implications regarding digital archives of spoken language

In the framework of programmes for documenting endangered languages such as those funded by the Volkswagen Foundation and the Arcadia Fund, unprecedented amounts of audiovisual data on endangered languages and cultures from around the world are currently being electronically archived. The expectation is that the materials collected will be more readily available (and for much longer) than previously, and available in ways that would benefit a number of different groups of potential users, including speakers who want to revitalise their languages and cultures. However, as I have argued elsewhere (Widlok 2010), the new electronic archives are not simply a quantitative extension of existing modes of data collection, but they qualitatively alter the relationship between researchers and their products and, as a consequence, also the relations between the researched and these products and the relationship between researchers and their partners in the field. The new possibilities of Internet-based digital archiving and online databases are much more than "just technical" innovations. Rather, the new archiving technology is also changing the ways in which we generate and share knowledge. The first half of this paper, therefore, aims to lay out

DOI: 10.111647/OBP.0032.02.

in some detail what is implied in the broad processes of electronic data gathering, digitisation, and online archiving.

Breathing life into data cemeteries

One of the most prominent assurances of new digital archiving technologies is that it can help to prevent data loss and data cemeteries. In the past, many recordings of spoken language have effectively been lost, not only materially but also through being buried in personal archives. The problem continues into the present and, arguably, it has been aggravated since the costs of recording have dropped dramatically. For myself and many colleagues, a major incentive to engage with digital archiving was to seek a strategy for coping with an ever-increasing private collection of audio- and videotapes, originating from various research projects over the years, materials for which it became ever more difficult to find a machine that would allow the data to be used in the future. Increasingly, there are also recordings, usually audio tapes, produced and kept by members of the speech community, but they frequently get recorded over after a while or are lost in closed collections. Field researchers tend to keep their data, but this data often ends up in data cemeteries, boxes of tapes awaiting transcription and translation. The prospects for these private collections are rather bleak: data loss due to media deterioration or due to the decommissioning of research projects and careers. My personal motivation for getting involved with the endangered languages programme DOBES (Dokumentation bedrohter Sprachen) of the Volkswagen Foundation, was the hope that the audio-visual data that I had accumulated in years of field research with ≠Akhoe Hai//om in northern Namibia could be prevented from deterioration and could be made accessible to others. After several years of running the project, many of my old tapes are now digitised and archived, but at the same time many more tapes have been added so that the total amount of untranscribed and unanalysed data is actually greater than what I started with. Moreover, the data collection has changed in ways that I had not anticipated when I began digital archiving. While I initially treated archives as passive "dumping grounds" it soon became clear that the digital archive was striking back, prompting me to reconsider basic assumptions and to change some of the habitual ways of doing research. The storage technology changed the record and changed the method of data gathering in at least three different ways, namely in terms of a departure from earlier holistic approaches, by fostering modularity and through the introduction of standardised metadata.

Farewell to holism

The composition of teams that make up documentation projects funded by the research initiatives already mentioned above is typically heterogeneous. The interdisciplinary teams include anthropological and linguistic researchers at a number of different levels (post-doc, PhD, research assistants, interpreters etc.) and for different time periods (short contracts, PhD projects, and as part of lifetime engagements). Since all members contribute to the data collection in different ways and at different times, the result is an open corpus very unlike the typical ethnographic monograph or conventional linguistic collection of folk-stories that tend to be holistic if not in scope then at least with regard to the fact that they are presented as a book or a similarly bounded entity. Ideally, the new digital corpora are supposed to grow even after the funding period has ended as researchers add to it and work on it for their various projects, and to various degrees this ideal is in fact realised. The corpus is eventually shaped not only by the original team of researchers but also by collaborators and by interested colleagues whose actions shape at least part of the corpus as they use it for a variety of purposes. This new set-up destroys any illusion that one might have had as the author of an ethnographic monograph or linguistic text collection in terms of holistic completeness and closure. On the positive side of things, the digital corpus more honestly reflects the fact that any field research is a long-term process of accumulating and revising knowledge, a process that tends to be hidden in the production of books and volumes. However, it remains to be seen how many of the newly established corpora will indeed become living bodies instead of turning into yet larger data cemeteries. Given that the funding agencies guarantee to keep the data collection active for decades (by migrating data to readable formats in the future), the chances are that we will see some interesting developments concerning the social life of data files. An inevitable trade-off in this development is that researchers partly lose control over the end product and, potentially, so do their informants. The researcher may be able to discuss publications with informants before they get printed, and will seek consent before things are recorded and put into an archive, but there is no way that a constantly growing and changing body of data that is subject to collective work and revision could be controlled in the same way. I shall return to this point in the second half of this chapter.

Welcome to modularity

It is tempting to look at digital archives as open-ended corpora that do away with the limitations of former collections of texts as indicated above. However, this primary openness should not be confused with amorphousness. For an electronic archive of spoken language to work, at least in the current set-up provided by electronic archiving software, it has to be organised in modules, usually called "sessions". These sessions are the basic units of data storage in electronic corpora. They can range from tiny one-sentence recordings to hours of videoed ceremonies and story-telling events. Moreover, the system allows for (and even encourages) any one recording to be organised in more than a single session, but the recording must minimally be part of one session (with metadata) in order to be visible in the corpus. The hypertext structure of the archive allows the underlying digitised tapes to be cut and joined in as many different ways as those working with the corpus care to specify. In our own project, for instance, we envisage that a healing dance that lasts several hours will form one session as a dance event, but that sections from this dance may also form separate sessions. In another example (see Widlok 2010: 51), a folk storytelling event may form a session of trickster stories, of cooperative story telling or of mother-in-law taboo since the underlying event is each of these three, namely a young man and his mother-in-law jointly narrating a trickster story.

Moreover, some projects have already experimented with community platforms that sort and present the data sessions not in terms of the categorical system of comparative linguistics or comparative anthropology, but in terms of what community members have found to be a useful organisation for their specific local purposes. In our own project, we have seen the beginnings of this in the use of sessions for community purposes: a common problem with largely egalitarian groups such as the ≠Akhoe Hai// om is that members do not easily speak for the community. When they get invited to represent their community at meetings in the capital, they tend to say little out of fear of getting criticised for what they have said when they return. This uneasiness to speak for others can be softened by using electronically archived materials. At one recent NGO-run workshop in the capital, the group members attending were showing video-clips (sessions from interviews) with voices from their home place. This allowed for more voices to be heard at the meeting without the delegate being forced to represent others in the context of their own established social practice that does not operationalise representing others as it is required by government or non-governmental organisations. Until recently, anthropologists (or other intermediaries) have often felt pressed to take over the role of speaker for the local community in these situations. Now they can take on the less contentious role of facilitators who only provide the technical equipment for what one may call a local appropriation of the archived materials.

The versatility of sessions as data clips is well established since *YouTube* and other Internet platforms have become ubiquitous sources. What is occasionally overlooked is the extent to which the often diffuse complexity of speech events and of ethnographic situations in which language is spoken becomes modularised with hard and fast boundaries so that we take these models to be true representations of the events from which they originate. In other words, there is a danger that the holistic illusion of a complete corpus that is dismantled in electronic corpora (see above) gets re-established at the level of sessions. In principle, there is no reason why we should not continue to cut new sessions from the original digital media files as we continue working, but in practice, the sessions—once established—tend to take on a life of their own.

Better data with meta-data?

Just as an organisation of the corpus in terms of sessions seems inevitable in the context of digital archiving, the same holds for the creation of metadata files that organise the data itself. To begin with, the sheer size of the data collections discussed here makes metadata essential. There is no easy way to find relevant cues if one has to go through hours of audio or video recording unless there is metadata that provides hints on the contents of the recording. Other minimally required metadata includes information about who collected, cut and processed the recording. Metadata is the main channel whereby context is preserved in terms of who said what, to whom, and in what kind of setting. As soon as the material leaves the confines of a private archive under the control of a researcher who can comment on the circumstances and details of the recording, and as soon as it reaches a public archive with considerable longevity, metadata is critical for contextualisation.

Correspondingly, archivists present metadata as the most critical resource for preventing the small data cemeteries mentioned above from being merged into huge data cemeteries. At this stage it becomes clear that, even with direct community involvement in compiling the corpus, digital archiving does not comply to the ideal of a dialogical research exercise with no power differentials. Clearly, the researchers who formulate the metadata (specifying participants, location, genres etc.) and the archivists who provide the templates for the metadata (controlled vocabularies, drop-down menus, boxes to be filled in) very much determine how sessions are described and corpora are compiled. Having said that, this of course is also true for many, if not all, data compilations that field researchers have hitherto come up with, be it text, audio, video or other. Context can never been exhausted, and there is always a selection of context. Whatever effort is made to make local voices heard, choices about the compilation and composition of the record usually remain with the researcher. The difference, compared to earlier practice, is that the metadata requirements of electronic archives render it necessary for the researcher to make his or her system of contextualisation open and explicit; and to agree with others on some shared standard. We all categorise our information (and to some extent our informants do that, as well) in one way or another, and similarly the events and situations from which the data is being derived. The metadata files in the corpora discussed here make it necessary to be explicit about these categorisations. Many researchers who are devoted to a particular language (and language community) are uneasy about the standardised categorisations of metadata descriptions. In any case, metadata specifications provide the opportunity to reflect on these categories. A major gap in the metadata that we found in our own project (see Widlok, Rapold and Hoymann 2008) is that the person-related information is usually individualised. Considerable effort is made in electronic archives to allow for a number of ways of anonymising speakers as individuals. However, the effort to connect the person-related information into a network (for instance of kin-relations between speakers) is still in its infancy. The metadata currently provides a purely summative list of informants and, as yet, no knowledge about the participatory frameworks in which data was generated.[1] In other words, research projects at present give information about individual contributors, but not about the social links between

---

[1] For the importance of participatory frameworks for understanding spoken language see William Hanks (1996: 142).

them. "KinOath", a new piece of software currently in development by Peter Withers at the Max Planck Institute for Psycholinguistics in Nijmegen, aims to close that gap. It is closely integrated with the "Arbil" metadata management tool.

An analysis of property and access rights regarding digital archives of spoken language

Digitisation not only affects the process of data collection and research but also the possibilities and limitations of access to that data. I am here not concerned with the (important) questions of access to digital technology and Internet connection—which continues to be a problem in many parts of the world—but rather those issues of regulating and managing access that, typically, linguists and anthropologists are expected to solve. Technically, the question of access rights to the collected data is solved in the sense that the archive allows researchers to categorise their data into different levels of access. Funding agencies like the Volkswagen Foundation would like the default level to be set at open and public so that all data (and not just the metadata) is openly accessible unless a specific reason is given to make it a temporarily restricted source. In fact, most project teams tend to see it the other way around. They open up very few selected show pieces for which there is open access. The largest part of the body is limited access with two thresholds: the lower threshold consists of an automatised declaration with which the user must agree along similar lines as agreements to Internet downloads and other web services. Instead of agreeing to a licence agreement, the user here agrees to have read the DOBES code of conduct and to comply with it in terms of protecting local communities and their intellectual property rights. The next threshold is that interested users have to get in touch with a responsible corpus manager (typically a member of the research team) who can then advise the archivist to grant them access to selected sessions from the corpus. Typically, this allows fellow researchers to make use of the corpus while the research team maintains some control over who uses the data. Closed access only exists as a temporary measure that is taken to grant researchers, especially PhD students, a period of exclusive use rights until they have completed their degree or publication. As I have pointed out elsewhere (Widlok 12–13 June 2008), these uniform and clear-cut technical access categories are in stark contrast to issues of property rights that are in most cases overlapping and of access rights that are typically shared, especially with regard to the long-term perspective.

The point to highlight here is that what changes with regard to earlier processes of granting or delimiting access is that we are no longer dealing with a dyadic negotiation between researcher and researched. Rather, there are now more parties involved: the funding agencies, with their open access policies but also, potentially, community agencies, often following restrictive practices and potentially in conflict with one another about who is the legitimate holder of the rights of the community. This raises the thorny issue of "group rights" and "cultural property" (see Barry 2001). We have seen conflicts of this sort arise over the repatriation of ancestral bones and artefacts to present-day indigenous communities and this suggests that similar problems may arise with electronically archived materials, especially when individual informants (and the responsible researchers) are no longer alive. While there is a need to specify access rights in the metadata, it is an illusion to think that this sufficiently accommodates for the complexity of rights issues. A first step towards solving many questions about property, I maintain, is to recognise at what level rights are actually claimed. In most cases property is made up of a bundle of rights (of ownership, of access, of use, of alienation, of inheritance) so that the recognition of authorship need not imply rights at other levels (as any author of a scientific publication knows).

A layered model of property and access rights

Many conflicts and misunderstandings surrounding property rights in data result from the fact that different layers of property rights are not sufficiently distinguished. For the purposes of this chapter we may distinguish layers concerning 1) values, 2) regulations, 3) relations, and 4) practices. For instance, we may all agree on certain values (such as the protection of privacy and the openness of scientific results) but there may still be debate about what kinds of regulations are best suited to realise these values, especially if more than one value is to be considered. Apart from that, there are discrepancies that may arise between different layers that make up complex property rights. I therefore suggest to apply to digital archiving of spoken language a layered model of property relations that has been developed in legal anthropology (see Benda-Beckmann and Benda-Beckmann 1999; and Widlok 2001). This model looks at property as a bundle of rights at the level of values, regulations, relations and practices. While language documentation programmes tend to be fairly outspoken about layers of values and regulations, they are less explicit about layers of social relationships and practice.

Cultural values of access

In a sense, cultural values of access is the most unproblematic layer of property rights, since there are a number of existing documents — developed after long discussions within the scientific community — that can be referred to. The DOBES Code of Conduct (CoC) has been discussed extensively in this regard; it also includes references to other existing codes.[2] Note that there are tensions built into all these codes since some values are at least potentially in conflict with one another, e.g. the right of privacy and the right of access to scientific results. This is the normal state of affairs and therefore we should not shrink back from embracing these values, even if they are partly in conflict with one another. This is why we need to look at the other layers, which can take the sting out of these tensions.

Each individual documentation team can refer to the relevant values that are formulated in documents such as the code of conduct, i.e. the respect towards intellectual and cultural property rights, the privacy of individuals, and the obligation to make the material accessible to interested non-commercial uses. However, even if we assume that there will be no changes in these values in the long-term future, inevitably, existing tensions between values will be resolved in different ways at various points in time. The current tendency is clearly towards open access. However, with increasing commoditisation, and possibly with the increasing disappearance of languages, the tendency may shift towards restricting access. The community of researchers now considers cultural heritage a treasure, but to some it may become a burden, too. The value of archiving may itself change in the future. It is not possible to foresee these developments, since our knowledge increases as language documentation grows. With spoken language materialising into data sessions and corpora

---

2   For a list of relevant documents, see International Association of Sound and Audiovisual Archives (IASA)'s *Copyright & Other Intellectual Property Rights* and The Hans Rausing Project for Endangered Languages' *Online Resources for Endangered Languages. Ethical issues* in Online Sources.

we may securely assume that the same dynamics are likely to emerge, that anthropology has found to be implicated in "the social life of things" (Appadurai 1986) in other domains of materialised culture. Given the longevity of data collection, many more conflicts become possible that did not apply when records of spoken language were more fleeting. As access rights will no longer be established once and for all but may change, these changes will have to be traced. In concrete terms, this means that a time-tag is added to every step in the digital archiving process, not just when setting up the metadata but with every change made to the access regulations. In an archive of "data objects" that can become subject to conflict, we need to know who made which access decision, when, and for how long it is to be effective.

Cultural regulations

The cultural values of access are operationalised into regulations by the teams running digital archives (in consultation with researchers). In the DOBES framework, there are a number of forms and rules such as the Usage Request Form (DOBES-UR), the Depositor-Archivist Agreement (DOBES-DAA) and Usage Declaration (DOBES-UD), as well as the Data Access and Protection Rules (DOBES-DAPR), which cover many aspects of what needs to be regulated with the help of forms.

The forms mentioned comprise some fundamental rules such as "all metadata [and all software] is openly accessible" and "by default, all archived materials [...] are not openly available and access therefore will be restricted" (DOBES-DAPR) as well as the more detailed rules as to what the conditions and procedures are for gaining access. It is noteworthy that at this layer, too, there are inbuilt tensions. For example, with regard to the notion of *shared* property and access rights according to which the copyright rests with both depositors and consultants (e.g. speakers), one can easily imagine situations where among depositors, among consultants or between these groups there may be conflicting interests. The regulations cannot and will not solve this problem for all possible constellations because these very much depend on what happens at the other layers (relations and practices, see below). At this point, the depositors are said to "always have unrestricted access" while the recorded persons have "a right to access" (DOBES-DAPR). In other words, the depositors have the privileged right of access for a maximum of three years and the privilege to formulate the access rights. The consultants have the privilege to allow or veto any commercial uses of the corpus material (a rule contained in the CoC). These rights are usually already contained in the research agreement that each DOBES project presented before research began. In the ≠Akhoe Hai//om case, this is a contract with one of the local non-governmental organisations. The contract, originally a contract for the media, was adapted in a way that it states:

1. Joint ownership held by the community of ≠Akhoe Hai//om speakers, the individual consultants, and the authors (in resulting publications)
2. The non-commercial nature of the project
3. Reference to the DOBES Code of Conduct
4. The fact that only openly accessible data will be collected

Note that while these regulations clarify the different *types* of rights that make up the whole bundle of rights that we cover under the term "property", they often pre-suppose that the *holders* of these rights are clearly defined. This is the weak point in most regulations of this sort, since the "community of speakers" is a vague concept, at best, and an outright fictional "body", at worst. Community organisations are known to be highly flexible and prone to conflict, fission and faction fighting. Projects should be aware that "the creators" or "the consultants" are not the same as the organisations with whom the contract has been made. As the case may be, a project team may draw up contracts with different bodies (just as consultants may enter into a contract with more than one research team). In the ≠Akhoe Hai//om case, we have a contract with a national NGO but we could have entered at the same time into contract with the national archive or the national university, and we have tried (so far unsuccessfully) to have yet another contract by creating a local voluntary interest group of people who have an interest in the corpus. If there are conflicts between individuals and organisations (or among organisations), there is no way that any such a contract and its regulations can prevent language documentation to be drawn into these conflicts. The best that one can hope for is that, on the basis of the Code of Conduct, language documentation does not create *new* conflicts, and that it does not lend itself easily for one faction or interest group to dominate others. The contracts or agreements should not create the illusion that with these regulations in place conflicts are eliminated. Rather, good contracts do not confuse the rights of all individuals concerned with the specific rights of the representative groups mentioned in contracts. Although a contract is typically a bilateral agreement (in terms of signatures), it can nevertheless be written as a three-party agreement between researcher, counterpart and the speakers, thereby recognising the difference between individual consultants and the organisations that claim to represent the community. In all likelihood, some third party, be it future researchers or speakers, will be affected by the agreements made. Even the so-called "final access statement" (to be made at the end of funding) is not really final insofar as a review of access rights is possible at regular intervals (every two years, see DOBES-DAA). This applies primarily to the distinction into three levels of access (open, on request, not accessible). Passwords that allow access to digital archives are given limited lifetimes (see DOBES-DAPR). Although there is a general tendency in archiving for resources to open up as time goes by (as the collection survives individuals, for instance), there is no categorical reason why access should not also be tightened up after a while, for instance if abuse has been occurring. Researchers and consultants could take advantage of the fact that regulations can be created with some sort of inbuilt shelf life date by which past decisions have to be reconfirmed or revised as a consequence of evolving social relations.

Social relations

It is important to recognise that some aspects relating to property issues cannot be covered with the help of regulations and forms (and in fact need not, or are better not, covered using these forms). For instance, we need to recognise that many statements about property and access rights in digital records of spoken languages are not necessarily about the relation between person or community and corpus. It may have much more to do with the relationship between community and person (e.g. the researcher) or between communities (e.g. speakers of a neighbouring variant). In other words, the lesson from the ethnography of property rights is that people often make property claims not because they necessarily want or need exclusive access to data, a particular recording for instance, but because they want to shape their relationship with others. Property and access claims signal to the rest of the world that local people want to be treated as equal, sovereign and autonomous in their decisions. These social aspirations are only partly satisfied by the use of forms and regulations. More often they are appropriately recognised and satisfied when complemented by other, more culturally sensitive modes of recognition. In its simplest form these are notes of recognition written by the researchers and covering not just the community of speakers but also, for instance, government ministries that provided research permits and any other stakeholder who has helped in the research. There are other means, some of which are already in use by language documentation projects. Publishing non-academic texts is one such way that shapes social relations. They are not just spin-offs from what we actually do but they are directly implicated in the social relations of property rights, and therefore should be considered an integral part of any language documentation. Another means is the installation of regional data servers which allow communities with restricted Internet access to use the corpus locally and, at the same time, functions as an important step in appropriately locating due recognition.

The recognition of the social relations layer can be both a relief and a challenge. It can be a relief in that it is open to creative ways of recognition beyond the signing of contracts. In some contexts the cultural standing of signed papers may be much lower than (or in any case complemented by), say, the presence of researchers at relevant events and occasions or their engagement for the community of speakers in other ways, for instance in dealings with the media or other outside agencies. At the same time, it can also be a challenge, in that it is simply not good enough to argue "we have signed the appropriate papers" and therefore assume that everything that needs to be done has been done. Contracts defining property rights not only define the relation between people and things (e.g. the corpus), but above all relations between people and other people.

Digital archives with Internet access face the additional practical problem of restricting something once it is out in the public domain. It is quite possible to imagine a situation in which materials, despite being technically accessible, become factually impossible to use because they would harm relationships. For instance, while researchers tend to assume that privacy rights decrease with time (as persons die), this may not be universally true, as — in many other contexts — people do not want unrestricted viewing of images relating to deceased members of their community. Even if copies of the images were already out in the open, it may be considered an impossibility to include them in displays or as examples in publications. More generally, people who may have agreed (even with their signature) to have material on public display may change their mind as they begin to realise what the Internet is and what open access may imply. Although they may not have any contractual (legal) basis for enforcing restrictions, researchers will no doubt consider accommodating these reservations in order to maintain a good working relationship. At the same time, honouring the decision of a speaker is different from honouring a decision made by a descendent of that speaker. In other words, there is no automatism that would grant a descendent of any contributor to the corpus the same rights as the contributor him- or herself held. They are in different positions to one another and with regard to the corpus. As access rights are handed on (possibly over generations), they may be subject to revision. There have to be default procedures for regulating access in the long term, but these have to be necessarily preliminary in the sense that they do not exist independently of the social relationships that do change over time.

Social practice

Finally, there is a layer of property relations which ultimately falls under the responsibility of each researcher and which will vary not just between field sites, but also between researchers. Many researchers who have worked with the same people for two decades have an informal agreement with people in the field. The collaborators in the field, in turn, then have a fairly good idea what the research is all about and are able to clearly signal when to switch off the camera or recorder if they want something to be off record. In fact, many researchers who have reached these means of understanding and agreements, whether tacit or explicit, which argue that—at the layer of practice—these often work just as well or even better than any written form of consent. However, there are other places and other situations, for instance with newcomers to the field or new people to be included as informants, where these agreements do not suffice. The problem is that only those who know the field and the people concerned will be able to tell and to decide on the appropriateness of formal regulations in actual practice.

It is important to note, however, that the practice layer of rights is of equal importance to all other layers. It is obviously not acceptable to use consent forms when one has—in practice—got the signature through subtle forms of cheating or bribery (giving of gifts) or through ignorance (not fully explaining its purpose). But then: who can fully guarantee that the counterpart has fully understood the implications of a piece of spoken language being included in a digital archive that is widely accessible? Are we, as researchers, able to see all future implications? Here it is highly relevant to include in the metadata what the research practice was like. To some, this kind of narrative may seem chatty or not part of the documentation proper, but I would contend that it is. Somewhere in the metadata, the future users of the archived materials should read not only about the stimuli for elicitation or recording tools that were used, but also a brief characterisation of how contact was established and what the everyday research practice looked like. This kind of information will, no doubt, be highly valued when anyone in the future wants to put the documentation into perspective. It is ultimately down to the individuals involved to include (or not to include) certain items in the documentation. Since individual researchers differ in the ways in which they restrict access to a source that he or she has collected, it is important to clearly mark who made decisions of access, and preferably also why.

Digitisation and electronic archiving are themselves not neutral activities, and there are a number of different ways in which researchers (and the researched) may want to integrate these activities into their own actions. The digital promise is that the language corpora will live on for much longer than if they were not digitised, and that they will continue to grow and improve in the future. However, after some years of experience in digital archiving (reflected in this chapter), we need to realise that digital archiving not only creates new problems, but also that some of the old problems, of data access for instance, will continue. For one, we cannot guarantee that the practices that we put in place now will remain unchanged. If we did that, then the corpus would be basically dead, a body in the true sense of the word. The power of large-scale electronic collections, such as those we see growing at this moment in time, is that they go beyond the single efforts and capacity of individual researchers. The downside of this is that each researcher only has limited influence on the overall product over time. The regulatory powers are much more constrained than in a traditional single-authored data collection such as a grammar, word list or collection of texts.

Every discipline has its early adapters who embrace the new recording devices while others attempt to cling to other formats that appear to be more holistic, easier to manage and easier to adapt to local requirements. What I have suggested in this chapter is that researchers across the whole spectrum need to realise that the new technologies do not solve problems of access or contextualisation, but rather shed a particularly sharp light onto these problems, which can be a first necessary step towards addressing the issues at hand.

The new archiving effort is, to a considerable extent, being driven by the new technology of documentation and of archiving. The archivists and the technical groups involved insist that regulating access to the digital resources, as well as how to best organise these corpora, is not their responsibility, but that it remains that of the researchers in close cooperation with representatives of those who contributed to the data corpus. While this initially promises a new and wider scope for providing and sharing data with communities, it also creates some enduring problems for the researchers involved. Archiving technology is indeed changing in some fundamental ways how we generate and share knowledge. The electronic online archive is not a container that passively waits to be filled with data. Rather, it also acts as a prompt and feeds back into the research process. In this chapter, I have suggested that analysing this prompt in terms of particular features of digital records and in terms of layers of property rights facilitates orientation when participating in this complex enterprise.

References

Appadurai, Arjun, ed., *The Social Life of Things: Commodities in Cultural Perspective* (Cambridge: Cambridge University Press, 1986).

Barry, Brian, *Culture and Equality: An Egalitarian Critique of Multiculturalism* (London: Polity, 2001).

Benda-Beckmann, Keebet and Franz von Benda-Beckmann, 'A Functional Analysis of Property Rights, with Special Reference to Indonesia' in *Property Rights and Economic Development*, ed. by Toon van Meijl and Franz von Benda-Beckmann (London: Kegan Paul, 1999), pp. 15–56.

Hanks, William, *Language and Communicative Practice* (Boulder: Westview, 1996).

Widlok, Thomas, 'Relational Properties: Understanding Ownership in the Namib Desert and Beyond', *Zeitschrift für Ethnologie*, 126 (2001), 237–268.

—, 'Property and Access Rights to the Corpus, Again', paper presented at the *DOBES (Dokumentation bedrohter Sprachen) Workshop at the Max Planck Institute for Psycholinguistics* (12–13 June 2008).

—, 'Bringing Ethnography Home? Costs and Benefits of Methodological Traffic across Disciplines' in *Ethnographic Practice in the Present*, ed. by Marit Melhuus, Jon P. Mitchell and Helena Wulff (London: Routledge, 2010), pp. 42–55.

—, Christian Rapold and Gertie Hoymann, 'Multimedia Analysis in Documentation Projects: Kinship, Interrogatives and Reciprocals in ≠Akhoe Hai//om', in *Lessons from Documented Endangered Languages*, ed. by David Harrison, David S. Rood and Arienne Dwyer (Amsterdam: Benjamins, 2008), pp. 355–370.

Online Sources

DOBES, *CoC Code of Conduct, UD Usage Declaration, UR Usage Request, DAPR Data Access and Protection Rules,* and *DAA Depositor-Archivist-Agreement*
<http://www.mpi.nl/DOBES/ethical_legal_aspects/>

DOBES homepage
<www.mpi.nl/DOBES>

International Association of Sound and Audiovisual Archives (IASA), *Copyright & Other Intellectual Property Rights*
<http://www.iasa-web.org/copyright-other-intellectual-property-rights>

Mark Liberman, *Web-Based Language Documentation and Description. Legal, Ethical, and Policy Issues Concerning the Recording and Publication of Primary Language Materials*
<http://www.ldc.upenn.edu/exploration/expl2000/papers/liberman/liberman.html>

The Hans Rausing Project for Endangered Languages, *Online Resources for Endangered Languages. Ethical issues*
<http://www.hrelp.org/languages/resources/orel/ethical.html>

Language Archive Technology, *Arbil Metadata Editor, Browser & Organizer Tool*
<http://www.lat-mpi.eu/tools/arbil/>

2. Access and Accessibility at ELAR, a Social Networking Archive for Endangered Languages Documentation

David Nathan

Discovering language documentation[1]

Language documentation, also known as documentary linguistics, is a subfield of linguistics that emerged in the 1990s as a response to predictions that the majority of human languages will disappear within a century (Krauss 1992). The discipline aims to develop "methods, tools, and theoretical underpinnings for compiling a representative and lasting multipurpose record of a natural language" (Gippert et al 2006: v). It weaves its focus on endangered languages together with traditional descriptive linguistics and a strong emphasis on the use of media and information technologies. It also encourages ethical practices such as involving language speakers as participants and beneficiaries (Grinevald 2003). Its central features are:[2]

---

1 The chapter focuses on access rather than usage, where usage is a cover term for several crucial and complementary issues such as intellectual property, copyright, privacy, and various kinds of usage licences. However, these are beyond the scope of this chapter. See Conathan (2011: 250) for an overview from an archive perspective; a good web source on these issues is Michael Brown's site *Who owns native culture?* (2012), please see Online Sources.

2 For further information, see Austin and Grenoble (2007), Himmelmann (2006: 15).

DOI: 10.111647/OBP.0032.03.

- *Focus on primary data*: documentation is based around collecting and analysing a range of primary language data
- *Interdisciplinarity*: documentation requires expertise from a range of disciplines, not just linguists. Its data should be available and accessible to a wide range of users
- *Involvement of the speech community*: collaboration with community members not only as consultants but also as co-researchers
- *Archiving*: materials should be preserved and made available to a range of potential users into the distant future

We can identify the participants and stakeholders in documentation as a prelude to considering what should be provided in terms of access. Firstly, there are the documenters themselves, typically linguists (and, occasionally, academics from other fields) who have received grants to do various kinds of documentation projects, together with the others in their teams who perform the various activities associated with running a project. Crucially, there are the language speakers and consultants, their families and communities. But not to be forgotten are the more peripheral stakeholders such as various institutions who host projects (typically universities) or are interested in evaluating the work or reputation of particular documenters, and governmental authorities interested in language planning. Finally—but most importantly when considering access issues—there are many categories of users: linguists and other researchers, teachers and applied linguists who are interested in resources for language revitalisation, heritage users (community members generally interested in resources related to their culture), journalists (who always want poignant stories about last speakers), and, finally, curious people who are interested in all kinds of "exotica".[3]

Typically, however, archives in our field have provided a narrow, one-way access strategy, enabling academic documenters to provide materials, and linguistic researchers to access them, as depicted in Figure 1 (Nathan and Fang 2009).

---

3   See also Woodbury (2011: 162, 177).

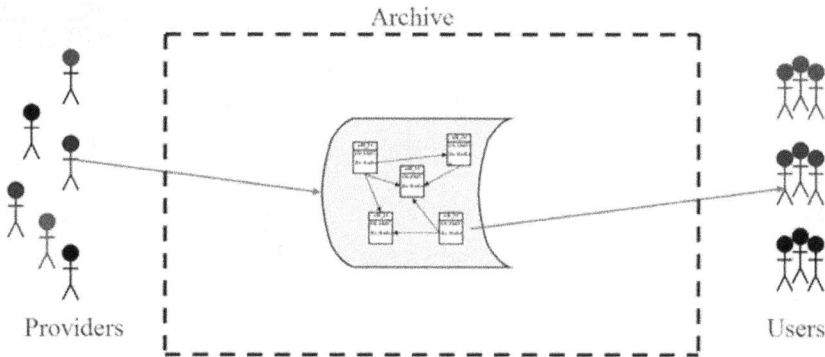

Figure 1.   Illustration of the narrow channel between documenters (providers) and linguists (users). Image by David Nathan, 2012.

From documentation to archiving

When policies and plans for the Endangered Languages Archive (ELAR) began to develop,[4] in around 2004,[5] documentary linguistics was not yet a mature discipline and its archiving needs were unclear. Even today, many of its basic parameters remain open to discovery rather than being fact or convention: "documentary linguistics is new enough [so] [...] that its scope, its scientific and humanistic goals, its stakeholders, participants and practices are still being explored and debated both inside and outside academic contexts" (Woodbury 2011: 171). We asked which aspects of documentation were both central to its practices and relevant to archiving and access. We were able to distil two such characteristics: diversity and protocol.

Himmelmann's seminal description of a language documentation as "a *multipurpose* [...] record of the linguistic practices characteristic of a speech community" (1998: 166; emphasis David Nathan) depicts its methods and outputs as inherently heterogeneous. Such records cannot then conform to a single template. Diversity is most clearly represented in the wide range

---

4   The ELAR in London, and its online catalogue is one programme of the Hans Rausing Endangered Languages Project, based at the School of Oriental and African Studies. ELAR's archiving activities are complemented by training, depositor support, outreach, and publishing.

5   ELAR opened in 2005 and launched its new catalogue system in June 2010.

of projects: ELDP's funded projects range from recording the "whistled language" of a tiny Amazonian community,[6] to a documentation of a language in China with thousands of speakers yet expected to decline quickly.[7] Layered on project contexts are their specific goals; whether, for example, they aim to describe particular linguistic phenomena, focus on annotated recordings, apply ethnomusicological understandings to songs, or create pedagogical resources for language revitalisation. Within each project, the cultures, communities and individuals with whom the documenter works all bring their unique skills, verbal styles, outlook, and motivations for participation. Documenters themselves are typically lone fieldworkers in remote locations (Austin 2005), so their practices are relatively unharmonised. Finally, of course, languages and their usages vary in yet unknown ways: that is what our awareness of language endangerment and the urgency of documentation tell us, for in truth we know relatively little about most of the world's 7,000 human languages.

Turning to the *forms* of documentations, there are few clear conventions for what actually counts as a language documentation (Himmelmann 2006: 10; Woodbury 2011: 171, 184). We find them containing a wide range of media, text types, and data formats, for which there are few agreed or settled standards; language data are not (yet) captured by an agreed framework of attributes. Compare this situation to that of libraries or businesses whose data is anchored in concepts such as title, author, page, quantity, cost, and item code all of which are well-established, stable, and correspond to real-world objects, rather than the contestable interpretations of linguistics. It is an open question as to whether a universal and stable set of concepts and categories will ever be formulated and agreed, although efforts are being made in that direction, e.g. GOLD Ontology, Leipzig Glossing Rules, and genre inventories (Johnson and Dwyer 2002).

The second key characteristic is *protocol*. ELAR uses this term as shorthand for the sum of processes involved in the formulation and implementation of language speakers' rights and sensitivities, and the consequent controlled access to materials. Protocol extends from the beginning of any documentation activity (e.g. when a documenter seeks informed consent from speakers, and then collects metadata on sensitivity

---

6 See Online Sources for Julien Meyer's project on the Gaviao and Surui languages, Documentation of Gaviao and Surui Languages in whistled and instrumental speech.
7 See Online Sources for Ross Perlin's project on the Dulong language, Documentation and description of Dulong.

and access from them for each recording) through to the mechanisms for providing, restricting, or negotiating about archived materials. To understand the pervasive importance of protocol for language documentation, consider that endangered language communities and their speakers are typically under various pressures and deprivations that are also contributing causes to the decline of their languages. These difficulties are amplified by the methodology of documentary linguistics, which most highly values the recording of spontaneous, natural speech. As languages cease to be spoken in a wide range of contexts (which is what primarily drives endangerment), people tend to use them more and more to speak of private, local, sensitive and secret matters. So the primary data of documentary linguistics maximises the likelihood of including content that can cause embarrassment or harm to the recorded speakers.[8]

A documentation archive

Archiving is an integral part of language documentation, for it would be pointless to document endangered languages without securing the safety and sustainability of the recorded data (Bird and Simons 2003). Today, several archives are devoted to endangered languages documentation.[9] Most of these are digital archives because documentation is inextricably linked with digital technologies in four ways: digital recording has made portable, high quality recording affordable; long term preservation of audio and video is possible only through lossless digital copying (IASA 2005); most researchers use computers to annotate media and create data and analysis in general; and the World Wide Web has become the ubiquitous platform for accessing documentation materials.

A digital documentation archive has to be more than a data repository. It has to find ways to preserve diverse materials and disseminate (or publish) them to a variety of stakeholders while safeguarding access where required. Most archives have collection policies (Conathan 2011: 240), some have policies which describe the types of access offered[10] or classes of users

---

8 In addition, documenters, unless they are community members, are likely to know less about sources of sensitivities—and are therefore less able to avoid them—than they might in other research contexts.
9 See Online Resources for a list on the Digital Endangered Languages and Musics Archive Network.
10 For example Peter Wittenburg (2005) Data Access and Protection Rules DAPR-V2, see Online Sources.

who they exist to serve,[11] however few explicitly link the architecture of their access system with the characteristics of their users. ELAR has done the latter by designing an archive with "Web 2.0" (also known as "social networking") features:

> [A]rchive access management can be effectively served and enhanced by the new [Web 2.0] technologies and the conventions that have quickly grown up around them. In Facebook [...] account holders build and participate in virtual communities by choosing who are to be their 'friends' — who are in effect the people who are permitted to see and interact with their presence on the site. In the same way, ELAR provides a channel for users to find and approach depositors to request access to materials, and for depositors to decide who will be their 'subscribers'. Distinct roles of audience/subscriber and author/depositor are at the heart of ELAR's design. (Nathan 2010: 122)[12]

In this design, the archive is reconceived as a platform for building, maintaining and conducting relationships between information providers and their users, just as many libraries see their mission as supporting learning rather than lending books.[13]

ELAR aims to "level the playing field" by offering more equitable access to various types of users rather than privileging the single-channel provision to researchers. We can cater better for language-speaker community members in several ways. The first is through our implementation of a nuanced protocol system to manage access and provide security and accountability. In Figure 1, green arrows show the workflow through a traditional archive; providers lodge their materials with the archive and users can (if permissions allow) find and access them. The archive functions as a searchable container for those materials. ELAR uses Web 2.0 interactivity to provide a dynamic access process. Depositors can edit metadata for their collection at any time, including the metadata that governs access. More importantly, the archive "plays out" protocol throughout its interface (see Figures 3–6), always letting users know which resources they can and cannot access, and offering a method for individual

---

11   See Online Sources for The Archive of the Indigenous Language of Latin America.
12   Although Facebook is used here to exemplify social networking, the newly released Google+ better resembles ELAR's model because it distributes a user's friends into "circles" just as an ELAR deposit provides various user roles; Facebook treats all a user's friends as a single group, see Online Sources.
13   See, e.g. Library Mission, Vission and Values, The University of Chicago Library (2004) in Online Sources.

access to otherwise restricted resources through direct application to the depositor (via "subscription"). A simplified representation of ELAR's subscription process is shown in Figure 2.

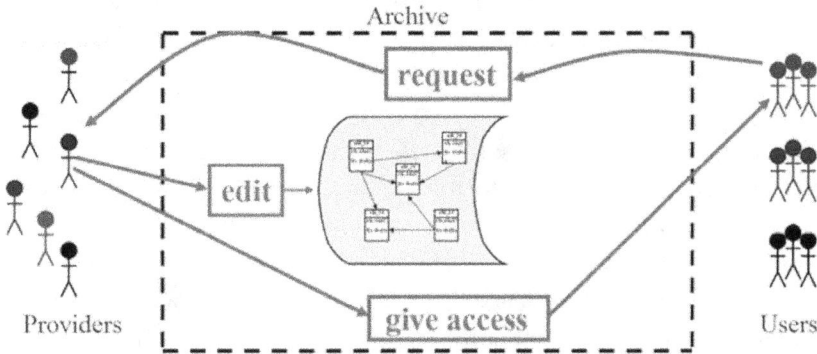

Figure 2.   Illustration of dynamic access via "subscription" at ELAR. Image by David Nathan, 2012.

URCS protocol roles

Before further outlining how ELAR's system works, I will describe its set of protocol roles. The protocol system is based around four roles (U, R, C and S) that have been defined as a result of research into depositors' preferences and through consultation with groups of depositors and archivists (Nathan 2010).

- U = ordinary User (must have an ELAR account)
- R = Researcher role
- C = Community member (protocol role) role (for a particular deposit only)
- S = Subscriber role (for a particular deposit or resource only)

Users are those people who have created an ELAR account. ELAR staff check account applications for bogus or scam attempts, but applications are in general automatically approved. Researcher role is available to relevant practitioners, for example linguists or teachers; applications for Researcher role are evaluated by ELAR staff and if approved apply across all collections in the archive.

Community member and Subscriber roles, however, are granted in relation to particular collections, and these applications are evaluated by the relevant depositor (or the depositor's delegate). A Community member is, as the name implies, someone recognised as a member of the language-speaker community. This category can also be used to set up other community-oriented categories such as a family, a set of individuals, or any other group that a depositor and his/her language consultants permit to access their data.[14]

A Subscriber is anyone who has identified a resource, requested permission to access it, and had their request approved by the depositor (see Figures 5 and 6). When a user submits a subscription request, the request is queued in the depositor's collection management panel. The depositor can see which item is being requested, together with information about the user (information that the user entered when they first registered for an account, including the user's identity, affiliation, and a statement about involvement with endangered languages). For further information, see ELAR's access protocol in ELAR's help system.[15] Depositors can also use the subscription system as a managed sharing mechanism (e.g. for limiting access to a project team).

The subscription system is a significant breakthrough in terms of broadening access to sensitive materials that in other archives would be under closed access. Subscription applications are channels for communication between owners and potential users of resources: in other words, users and depositors *gain access to each other*.

How protocol works

As users navigate the ELAR website, its management system matches the URCS values of the resources in focus with the URCS rights of the logged-in user. Anyone can view a collection home page (see Figure 3), and see a resource's metadata, but only logged in account holders can access ELAR resources. Although requiring accounts limits wider access to ELAR's open (U) resources, we think this is a cost worth bearing. As described above,

---

14   Currently, eligibility for access under Community member is decided by the depositor or depositor's delegate. We hope to develop a more flexible approach to managing this role in the future. The AILLA archive, for example, has a system using special passwords as answers to questions that only eligible community members would know, see Online Sources.

15   See Online Sources.

the subscription process supplies depositors with reliable information about requesters, including validated identities and archive usage history.[16] We do not support user anonymity; rather, we provide depositors with information about access of their collections. These components of a protocol system help to build and maintain a high level of trust and confidence on the part of depositors and their language consultants.

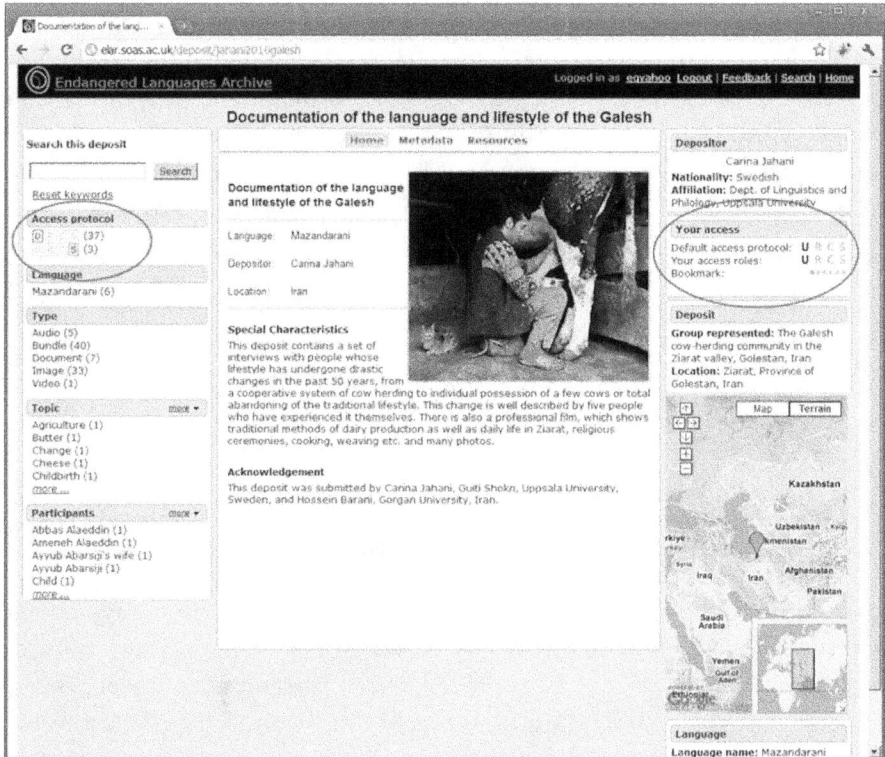

Figure 3.   Screenshot of ELAR home page for documentation of the language and lifestyle of the Galesh, Carina Jahani. Protocol labels and controls are circled. Image by ELAR/David Nathan, 2012.

As can be seen from Figure 3, we made a bold commitment to make protocol a prominent feature of the archive interface.[17] It inverts the navigational design of other archives where one searches and navigates to a resource

16   We are in the process of implementing some of these features.
17   Various web projects by Kimberley Christen and research partners have focused on interfaces for cultural protocols "that both limit and enhance the exchange, distribution and creation of knowledge". See Online Sources.

of interest, only to be faced by a "not available" message or a pop-up demanding a log in to an unknown service; users do not discover that a given resource is closed until having *completed* a possibly complex search. In such archives it can even be difficult for depositors themselves to know what access conditions currently hold for their own materials.

How does a user make use of ELAR's protocol information? Information at the top right of the collection's Home page (see Figure 3) provides an overview, showing the default access protocol for the collection, together with the default access rights for the presently logged-in user. For performing search/navigation, controls are provided in the navigation panel. These also give more information. Figure 4 shows the user that 37 resources are available (because "U" is outlined in solid green), while three Subscriber-only resources are unavailable (indicated by the "S" in dotted red outline).

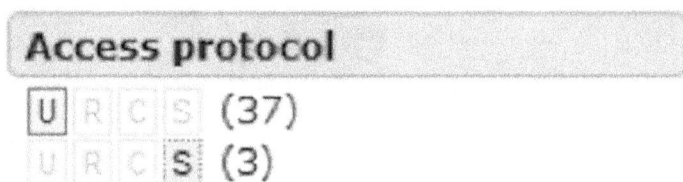

Access protocol

U R C S (37)
U R C S (3)

Figure 4.   Access protocol controls in the navigational panel in the ELAR website. Image by ELAR/David Nathan, 2012.

Users who only want to be shown resources for which they have access rights can thus search or browse by clicking on the appropriate protocol category. On the other hand, if a user browses all resources and reaches one which is Subscriber-only, he/she is offered an option to "Apply for access rights", which, if clicked, triggers the subscription application process described above.

▼ Documentation of the language and lifestyle of the Galesh

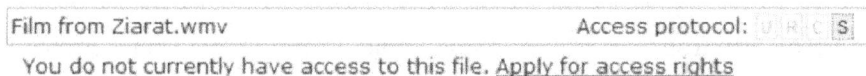

Film from Ziarat.wmv   Access protocol: U R C S

You do not currently have access to this file. Apply for access rights

Figure 5.   Display of a subscriber-only resource in the ELAR website. Image by ELAR/David Nathan, 2012.

After a subscription application is approved by the depositor, the user will see the "S" icon outlined in green, as shown in Figure 6, where a (different) resource is available, in this case an audio file which can be either played or downloaded.

▼ **Cornelio 2**

co_cornelio2.wav   Access protocol: U R C S

◀ ▶

download

Figure 6.   This user has subscription rights to this resource in the ELAR
           website. Image by ELAR/David Nathan, 2012.

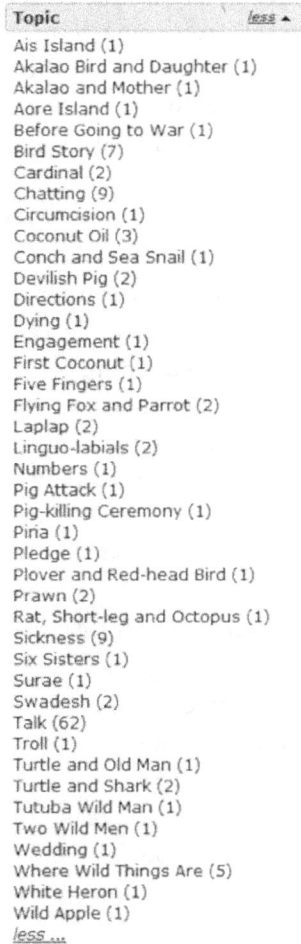

Topic	less ▲
Ais Island (1)	
Akalao Bird and Daughter (1)	
Akalao and Mother (1)	
Aore Island (1)	
Before Going to War (1)	
Bird Story (7)	
Cardinal (2)	
Chatting (9)	
Circumcision (1)	
Coconut Oil (3)	
Conch and Sea Snail (1)	
Devilish Pig (2)	
Directions (1)	
Dying (1)	
Engagement (1)	
First Coconut (1)	
Five Fingers (1)	
Flying Fox and Parrot (2)	
Laplap (2)	
Linguo-labials (2)	
Numbers (1)	
Pig Attack (1)	
Pig-killing Ceremony (1)	
Piria (1)	
Pledge (1)	
Plover and Red-head Bird (1)	
Prawn (2)	
Rat, Short-leg and Octopus (1)	
Sickness (9)	
Six Sisters (1)	
Surae (1)	
Swadesh (2)	
Talk (62)	
Troll (1)	
Turtle and Old Man (1)	
Turtle and Shark (2)	
Tutuba Wild Man (1)	
Two Wild Men (1)	
Wedding (1)	
Where Wild Things Are (5)	
White Heron (1)	
Wild Apple (1)	
less ...	

Users of this system are always aware of their access protocol context. They can choose to only search for accessible items, or they can request access to items where necessary. And at any point, users know *why they can or cannot access* particular resources.

Searching, browsing and metadata

So far I have described the role of protocol in navigating ELAR's resources. ELAR also provides search and browse functions. Its search is fairly standard, offering a stemmed search over all archive metadata.[18] ELAR places higher priority on enabling users to browse. Browsing reflects the diversity of documentation; with its wide array of resources, formats, and metadata, users need a way to find out what is available. Browsing provides a user-friendly "road map" rather than potential responses to specific queries. It is implemented using a dynamic "faceted browse" system, visible in the left hand panel in Figure 3; a detail for another collection appears in Figure 7.

Figure 7.   User-friendly discovery using faceted browsing in the ELAR
           website. Image by ELAR/David Nathan, 2012.

---

18 Stemmed search means that terms are searched according to their uninflected forms; for
    example, searching for "cats" will find all resources containing "cat" in their metadata
    and vice versa.

There are, of course, good arguments for providing search over standardised metadata—for example ISO 639 codes enable users to accurately find all resources for a certain language, despite the variety of names it might have.[19] Such strategies have been the backbone of traditional library and indexing practice. But it is important to remember that while they serve certain classes of users and purposes very well, they also diminish access to other users and purposes. Researchers, for example, are likely to know—or know how to find—standard codes for languages. Searches via such codes yield high recall (returning most of the relevant resources, not missing many) and high precision (returning relevant resources, with few irrelevant ones). However, for many of the users and purposes we wish to serve, query interfaces provide low recall due to their "ontological flatness" (Christie 2005: 13).

A non-researcher language community member, for example, is likely to get better results when looking for a story about a particular animal or place if they can see the names of the animal or place displayed, and even better results if the colloquial or language term for that animal or place is shown (rather than, say, the scientific or official name). Depending on the level of literacy in a community, even the colloquial or language terms may not normally be written, or may have variant spellings, so users are better supported by being able to browse and select rather than being forced to type in search strings.

Metadata underlies these searching and browsing functions. ELAR takes a permissive approach to metadata, encouraging each depositor to supply as rich and descriptive a set as possible (Nathan 2011). ELAR also attempts to expose as much as possible of this metadata. Examples can be seen in Figures 3 and 7, where topics include butter, cheese, and pigs. In other cases, terms in local languages, such as Kastom,[20] or phonetic terms and symbols appear.[21]

ELAR's approach "levels the playing field" in several ways. For example, if depositors provide names of the speakers/performers of recordings, these can be displayed for browsing on the collection's home

---

19   For example, Ethnologue lists 7,413 "primary" language names, but these have over 43,000 alternate (and dialect) names. However, many of theses names are exonyms (i.e. not the community's own term for their language).

20   See Online Sources for Documentation of Mavea, Valérie Guérin.

21   See Online Sources for Somyev (Sombə; KGT) Segmental and Tonal Contrasts, Bruce Connell.

page (see under "Participants" in Figure 3). Speakers now appear right "up front" in the interface; their status is represented similarly to that of the depositor. Community members—or others with no connection to the documenter or linguistic goals—can find and browse performances by those speakers, without having to remember the name of a fieldworker who once visited, the linguist's name for the project, or the ISO code for their language.

Access and accessibility

ELAR's approach to protocol, search, and browsing aims to enhance access, but we have not yet asked the question: what *counts* as access? Searching and browsing, and file display or download, are not ends in themselves. Ultimately, access has to take into account *accessibility to the content* of interest to users. Different people want different things. Depending on users' goals, and the content they desire, access could mean viewing metadata, playing an audio or video in the browser, or downloading a file to play or manipulate it later (see Figure 8). Formal linguists might want to download interlinearised marked-up material; community members might want to "click and play" recordings of songs, stories, and events; language planners or educationalists might want to assess the range and quality of the available resources.

Some people mistakenly look to in-browser delivery as a strategy to *prevent* users receiving a digital copy of a file. This confuses access to content with the apparatus that delivers that content.[22] Instead, we have to shift our focus from access to accessibility. Take, for example, someone with little technical interest in their Internet-connected computer who wants to learn a song. A simple "play" button will maximise the accessibility of the song. But someone who wants to acoustically analyse speech or transcribe it in specialised software like ELAN will not be able to do so without downloading.[23]

---

22 In these days of "always on" broadband, cloud computing, and a myriad of software for capturing YouTube media, in-browser media players are not a bulwark against file download or copying.

23 See Online Sources for The Language Archive: ELAN, Max Planck Institute for Psycholinguistics.

▼ **batusía chukú**

Figure 8.   Playing a video in the browser—is *this* access?[24] Screenshot from the ELAR website. Image by ELAR/David Nathan, 2012.

Providing accessibility goes beyond allowing a choice between playing and downloading; suitable renditions of content might need to be made for different audiences (Nathan 2006; Holton 2011). Not all users want, or can use, audio or video with time aligned morphological annotation. Eli Timan's ELAR collection includes time aligned morphological annotation,[25] but it is accompanied by a community resource that forgoes most of the "linguistic" content, and provides what Eli, as a community member himself, knows that they might use: transliteration in Arabic and translation into English, together with pictures drawn by the story teller.[26] Another alternative we are working on is an in-browser video player (see Figure 9) that uses speech bubbles, a very conventional (and therefore accessible) method to present the written content of a conversation.[27]

---

24   From the collection Choguita Rarámuri description and documentation, Gabriela Caballero (see Online Sources).
25   See Online Sources for Preservation of the Jewish Iraqi spoken language, Eli Timan.
26   See Online Sources for these materials at Jews of Iraq.
27   The speakers, conversing in Pite Saami, are Henning Rankvist (left) and Elsy Rankvist

Figure 9. Experimental speech bubble player. Note that the preferred orthography for Pite Saami has changed and the bubbles would now be written as follows: Henning: ja dä vuosjgunijd ja tjuovtjajd; Elsy: mikkir gulijd åtjojde? The speakers, conversing in Pite Saami, are Henning Rankvist (left) and Elsy Rankvist (right). Image by ELAR/David Nathan, 2012. Screenshot from the ELAR website, from an ELAR collection deposited by Joshua Wilbur, *Pite Saami: Documenting the Language and Culture*. The speech bubble player was created by Edward Garrett.

Perceptions and the interface

Accessibility also depends on users' perceptions. Much of this paper has been about the nature of an archive's user interface; its design, layout, interactivity, controls and navigation. While many of these factors are based on underlying functional decisions, the overall effect—often called "the user experience"—is greater than the sum of such decisions. Interface design plays a significant role in achieving goals. ELAR chose a contemporary

---

(right). From an ELAR collection deposited by Wilbur, Pite Saami: documenting the language and culture (see Online Sources). The speech bubble player was created by Edward Garrett.

look, echoing features of Facebook and blogs, because these genres reduce the perception of distance and power disparity, and encourage productive interaction (Bozarth 2010: 55). ELAR prominently signposts protocol throughout the website not only to guide users through the new interface,[28] but also to embody a commitment to depositors' protocol choices.

Sometimes things play out in unpredictable but serendipitous ways. Recently a researcher described a West African community's responses to some archive websites. The community has only recently been connected to the Internet, and they mainly use sites such as Facebook, for social purposes. So for them, a prototypical website looks and works like Facebook, and after being shown a few online archives, they judged that ELAR was the only "real" one.

Interfaces can be misleading. For example, archives may give a false perception of access control. Some linguists believe that a particular language archive does not allow downloading of files, although investigation revealed that it is quite possible to download from that archive. The opacity of the archive's interface makes it so difficult to accomplish a download that they had concluded that it was impossible. This situation disadvantages those who legitimately want to access materials and gives a false sense of security to depositors who imagine a level of control that does not exist. In this case, perceptions have conflated difficulty of access with control of access.

Interfaces can also be subtle and unpredictable. Nariyo Kono's documentation of Kiksht (Warm Springs, Oregon, USA) contained sensitive materials,[29] so they were deposited at ELAR under Subscriber-only access, available only to the depositor and the small community team she worked with. However, after the collection was accessioned and online, and the community members saw themselves displayed, they felt uncomfortable and wrote urgently to ask us to "turn off" access. I replied, explaining the benefits of them being able to see and check the site before allowing others to access it (or indeed to decide against access). However, I had misunderstood; the fact that they could see themselves appearing in the browser, on the screen—in the place where normally only "others" appear—was disturbing. We negotiated time to allow further discussion

---

28 ELAR's social-networking style interface is new to language archives, although it is borrowed heavily from the existing social networking genre (online resource discovery through querying standardised metadata).

29 See Online Sources for Conversational Kiksht, Nariyo Kono.

back in Warm Springs, and after a month the go-ahead was given to re-open the collection to community members only.[30]

The issue of access to archive resources is multifaceted, and goes far beyond designating resources as open or closed. I have illustrated some of the advantages of custom solutions for a specific field: here, endangered languages documentation. The central concept is a nuanced set of protocol values "URCS", of which two describe a relation between an individual user and a particular resource which is negotiated between the user and depositor. We have not yet encountered a case where these roles and their associated mechanisms did not provide an appropriate solution for the protocol needs of a depositor or community. In fact, we have been surprised at the number of apparently complicated cases that can be handled by the flexibility of the Subscriber role.

The response from depositors to ELAR's access system has been unanimously positive. Some have elected to deposit materials with ELAR that they would not deposit elsewhere, because our attention to protocol has inspired their trust. Others have approached ELAR for archiving as a result of searching for an archive with such a model for protocol and accountability. Some depositors who are preparing collections for deposit, on realising that ELAR can directly provide resources to the communities they work with, have reshaped their collections and revised their metadata to take advantage of the systems described here.

There is still much work to do. Depositors can edit the content of their collection Home page (Figure 3) to add translations in the documented language or a lingua franca,[31] but we would also like to be able to present the whole navigational interface in a variety of languages.[32] With our small team we do not have the resources to accomplish that, but some depositors have already offered to help. It would be great to complete the social networking dynamic by allowing users to contribute comments, links and materials, and to collaborate with depositors, but all of these moves will require careful consideration of moderation and protection of moral rights and intellectual property.

---

30 I am grateful to Nariyo Kono, Valerie Switzer, Radine Johnson, and Pam Cardenas for sharing their views of this experience with me, and I apologise for any errors or remaining misunderstandings.

31 For example, Shenkai Zhang has provided summary information in Chinese for her ELAR deposit; see Online Sources for Pingjiang traditional love songs.

32 AILLA, for example, enables users to toggle the entire interface between English and Spanish (see Online Sources).

Until now, access has more or less meant providing "insiders" with the means to locate specialist materials by using constrained ontologies. ELAR has sought to help "outsiders" to access content they hope to find or perhaps never imagined finding. In doing so we are replacing a "stork and baby" approach to archiving—deposit and abandon—with a platform for ongoing relationships and activities around the data. This does require an increased commitment on the part of depositors, but it will likely result in an enrichment of documentary linguistics and greater support for speakers of endangered languages.

References

Austin, Peter K., *Training in Language Documentation: The SOAS Experience*, unpublished paper presented at the Linguistics Society of America Conference on Language Documentation: Theory, Practice, and Values (Harvard University, 9–11 July 2005).

—, and Lenore Grenoble, 'Current Trends in Language Documentation', in *Language Documentation and Description, Vol 4*. ed. by Peter Austin (London: SOAS, 2007), pp. 12–25.

—, and Julia Sallabank, eds., *The Cambridge Handbook of Endangered Languages* (Cambridge: Cambridge University Press, 2011).

Bird, Steven and Gary Simons, 'Seven Dimensions of Portability for Language Documentation and Description', *Language*, 79(3) (2003), 557–582.

Bozarth, Jane, *Social Media for Trainers: Techniques for Enhancing and Extending Learning* (San Francisco: Wiley, 2010).

Christie, Michael, *Aboriginal Knowledge Traditions in Digital Environments*, (unpublished paper Charles Darwin University, 2005) <http://www.cdu.edu.au/centres/ik/pdf/CHRISTIE_AJIEpaper.pdf> [Accessed 24 October 2012].

Conathan, Lisa, 'Archiving and Language Documentation', in *The Cambridge Handbook of Endangered Languages*, ed. by Peter K. Austin and Julia Sallabank (Cambridge: Cambridge University Press, 2011), 235–254.

Gippert, Jost, Nikolaus P. Himmelmann and Ulrike Mosel, eds., *Essentials of Language Documentation Trends in Linguistics. Studies and Monographs*, 178 (Berlin: Mouton de Gruyter, 2006).

Himmelmann, Nikolaus P., 'Language Documentation: What Is It and What Is It Good For?'. In *Essentials of Language Documentation Trends in Linguistics. Studies and Monographs*, 178, ed. by Jost Gippert et al. (Berlin: Mouton de Gruyter, 2006), 1–30.

Holton, Gary, 'The Role of Information Technology in Supporting Minority and Endangered Languages', in *The Cambridge Handbook of Endangered Languages*, ed. by Peter K. Austin and Julia Sallabank (Cambridge: Cambridge University Press, 2011), 371–399.

IASA Technical Committee, *The Safeguarding of the Audio Heritage: Ethics, Principles and Preservation Strategy*, ed. by Dietrich Schüller, Version 3 (= Standards, Recommended Practices and Strategies, IASA-TC 03) (International Association of Sound and Audiovisual Archives, 2005) <http://www.iasa-web.org/tc03/ethics-principles-preservation-strategy> [Accessed 24 October 2012].

Johnson, Heidi and Arienne Dwyer, 'Customizing the IMDI Metadata Schema for Endangered Languages', in *Proceedings of The International Conference on Language Resources and Evaluation* (2002) <http://www.mpi.nl/lrec/2002/papers/lrec-pap-05-JohnsonDwyer.pdf> [Accessed 24 October 2012].

Krauss, Michael, 'The World's Languages in Crisis', *Language*, 68 (1992), 6–10.

Nathan, David, 'Thick Interfaces: Mobilising Language Documentation'. In *Essentials of Language Documentation Trends in Linguistics. Studies and Monographs*, 178, ed. by Jost Gippert et al. (Berlin: Mouton de Gruyter, 2006), 363–379.

—, 'Archives 2.0 for Endangered Languages: From Disk Space to MySpace', *International Journal of Humanities and Arts Computing*, 4.1–2 (2010), 111–124.

—, 'Better Data about Metadata: A Survey of Depositor Metadata Submitted to the Endangered Languages Archive', unpublished paper presented at the Annual Meeting of the Linguistic Society of America, Organized Session on Metadata (Pittsburgh, 7 January 2011).

—, and Meili Fang, 'Language Documentation and Pedagogy for Endangered Languages: A Mutual Revitalisation', in *Language Documentation and Description, Vol 6*, ed. by Peter Austin (London: SOAS, 2009), 132–160.

Woodbury, Anthony, 'Language Documentation', in *The Cambridge Handbook of Endangered Languages*, ed. by Peter K. Austin and Julia Sallabank (Cambridge: Cambridge University Press, 2011), 159–211.

Online Sources

The Archive of the Indigenous Languages of Latin America (AILLA)
<http://www.ailla.utexas.org/>

Michael Brown, *Who owns native culture?* (2012)
<http://web.williams.edu/go/native/>

Kimberley Christen's web projects
<http://www.kimchristen.com/projects.html>

Digital Endangered Languages and Musics Archive Network
<http://www.delaman.org/participants.html>

ELAR: The Hans Rausing Endangered Languages Project and School of African and Oriental Studies (SOAS, London), *Endangered Languages Archive*
<http://elar-archive.org>

ELAR, *Choguita Rarámuri description and documentation, Gabriela Caballero*
<http://elar.soas.ac.uk/deposit/caballero2009raramuri>

ELAR, *Conversational Kiksht, Nariyo Kono*
<http://elar.soas.ac.uk/deposit/kono2009kiksht>

ELAR, *Documentation of Mavea, Valérie Guérin*
  <http://elar.soas.ac.uk/deposit/guerin2007mavea>
ELAR help system
  <http://elar.soas.ac.uk/help>
ELAR, *Documentation of the language and lifestyle of the Galesh, Carina Jahani*
  <http://elar.soas.ac.uk/deposit/jahani2010galesh>
ELAR, *Preservation of the Jewish Iraqi spoken language, Eli Timan*
  <http://elar.soas.ac.uk/deposit/timan2008jewishiraqi>
ELAR, *Pingjiang traditional love songs, Shenkai Zhang*
  <http://elar.soas.ac.uk/deposit/ zhang2010pingjiang>
ELAR, *Somyev (Somba; KGT) Segmental and Tonal Contrasts, Bruce Connell*
  <http://elar.soas.ac.uk/deposit/connell2010somyev>
ELAR, *Pite Saami: Documenting the Language and Culture, Joshua Karl Wilbur*
  <http://elar.soas.ac.uk/deposit/wilbur2009pitesaami>
Ethnologue
  <http://www.ethnologue.com>
Facebook
  <http://www.facebook.com>
GOLD Community, *GOLD ontology*
  <http://linguistics-ontology.org/>
Google+
  <https://plus.google.com>
The Hans Rausing Project
  <http://www.hrelp.org>
Jews of Iraq
  <http://jewsofiraq.com>
The Language Archive: ELAN, Max Planck Institute for Psycholinguistics
  <http://www.lat-mpi.eu/tools/elan>
Max Planck Institute for Evolutionary Anthropology Department of Linguistics,
  Leipzig Glossing Rules
  <http://www.eva.mpg.de/lingua/resources/glossing-rules.php>
Julien Meyer, *Documentation of Gaviao and Surui Languages in Whistled and Instrumental Speech*
  <www.hrelp.org/grants/projects/index.php?projid=148>
Ross Perlin, *Documentation and Description of Dulong*
  <http://www.hrelp.org/grants/projects/index.php?projid=123>
The University of Chicago Library (2004), *Library Mission, Vission and Values*
  <http://www.lib.uchicago.edu/e/about/mvv.html>
Peter Wittenburg (2005) *Data Access and Protection Rules DAPR-V2*
  <http://www.mpi.nl/DOBES/ethical_legal_aspects/DOBES-access-v2.pdf>

3. Multiple Audiences and Co-Curation: Linking an Ethnographic Archive of Endangered Oral Traditions to Contemporary Contexts

Judith Aston and Paul Matthews

The fieldwork recordings

Unusually for an anthropologist of her generation, anthropologist Wendy James has been consistent in her use of audiovisual media in her fieldwork. She began this process in the mid-1960s, whilst working as a lecturer at the University of Khartoum, initially using silent cine footage, reel-to-reel audio, black and white photographs and colour slides to record interviews and document her observations. On subsequent visits, she has recorded on audio-cassettes, Hi-8 video and most recently taken photographs on a mobile phone.

Whilst initially making recordings for research and teaching purposes, to act as aide memoires to her written analytical work and to enliven her lectures, over the years James has come to recognise the wider relevance and value of these recordings. This is linked to the way in which her role in the field has been transformed. Initially, she went into the field as a participant observer working on her doctoral thesis under the supervision of the anthropologist Evans-Pritchard. However, in the mid 1980s, widespread fighting broke out in the region and this led to her becoming a historical witness of the effects of war and displacement on a marginal community. Subsequently, she has acted as a consultant for a television documentary

DOI: 10.111647/OBP.0032.04.

as part of the Granada Television's "Disappearing World" series on war (MacDonald 1993), and became a humanitarian advocate and report writer for various agencies working in the region.

In documenting aspects of James' intermittent fieldwork from the mid-1960s through to the present day, the recordings shed light on major world events in the latter half of the twentieth and early part of the twenty-first century, from the perspective of an anthropologist who has built a strong relationship over the years with her informants. These informants come primarily from the Uduk-speaking people of the Sudan-Ethiopian borderlands. Over the years, James has made it her business to become highly conversant in the language and has built friendships that go beyond the standard remit of shorter-term anthropological fieldwork. One does not have to spend long with her materials before this becomes apparent, with her written analyses also reflecting this deep engagement.

Whilst these recordings are inevitably framed by James' research interests as a professional anthropologist, they also offer insights into a period of African history as seen from the perspective of a minority people whose lives have been transformed by civil war and repeated displacements. Once living together in relatively stable rural hamlets, the Uduk-speaking people are now dispersed across national borders, with some living in countries as far afield as the USA. James' recordings reveal how the survival of a vernacular language can help to create a powerful network of overlapping memory and practice, through which old patterns and traditions can re-appear even in the most "modern" of circumstances.

Linking written analysis to fieldwork recordings

In her written ethnographies and associated papers about her fieldwork, James recognises that the personal stories of the handful of people that she knew well, and who helped her in her original research in the 1960s, "weave in and out of the whole tragedy of the Sudanese civil war and the deadly choreography of its entanglements with the struggles in Ethiopia" (James 1999 [1988]: xi-xii). She has always tried to write about the events and changes that have occurred as far as possible through the words and experiences of the people themselves and has expressed frustration that "the discussion of emotion, culture and language is greatly hampered by the format of written ethnography alone, and even by the written version of the recorded and translated vernacular" (James 1997: 124). It was this frustration that led her into collaborating with Aston, and which led to the creation of a website (Aston and James 2007) to complement her most recent book on her fieldwork (James 2007). In the preface to this book, she writes that the website is there to add "emotional tone and a sense of the character and personalities" of people quoted in the book (ibid: xix).

The book is the third of a trilogy and looks at the recent history of displacement in the region from the year in which the Sudan Peoples' Liberation Army (SPLA) was founded in 1983 up to the year of the Comprehensive Peace Agreement between the Sudan government and the SPLA of January 2005. Through the inclusion of personal testimony, it shows how the Uduk-speaking people, originally from the Blue Nile region between the "north" and the "south" of the Sudan, have been caught up in and displaced by civil war. Whilst some responded to the situation by defending their nation, others joined the armed resistance of the SPLA. Many found temporary security as international refugees in Ethiopia, whilst others opted for resettlement further afield in countries such as the USA. The book shows how the paths of those that have survived have converged and diverged in different places at different times, in such a way that there has not been a permanent severing of ties or cultural belonging. It shows how links have been maintained across borders and continents through modern communications and where possible through the recreation in new settings of traditional forms of storytelling, music and song.

The website contains a selection of songs, which are quoted in the book, as well as some maps of the region and a series of photographs that chart the journey of displacement from the rural hamlets of the 1960s to a semi-permanent refugee camp in Ethiopia by 1993. Its main component, however, is a series of thematically arranged video clips, which illustrate various kinds of instrumental music and dance referred to in the book and which give access to a number of interviews and conversations from the refugee communities in 1993 and 2000. These engage the viewer in the subjectivities of James' informants by showing their reflections on the past and their hopes for the future. The viewer can select to view a specific clip in the Uduk language alongside a summary in English of what is being said, with references to places in the book where James provides further context on the issues raised.

Although the website does include some footage from the 1960s, its focus is on the refugee situation prior to repatriation in 2007–08. Having completed this website, we are now planning a more ambitious project, closely linked to the creation of a digital archive of James' recordings. This project is to create an online presentation, which incorporates a wider range of her materials and is organised according to the principles of thematic and temporal navigation. This presentation will enable users to follow pre-authored pathways through the materials, whilst also allowing them to engage with materials in a more exploratory fashion. Whilst contextual commentary will initially be provided by James, user communities will be invited to respond to this commentary and to create their own additional pathways. Provision will also be made for James' informants to contribute their own recordings to the presentation, as a means of extending the narrative as they begin to document their own experiences.

Adding contextual commentary to fieldwork recordings

Having recently retired from departmental duties, James has now begun the process of organising and preparing her fieldwork recordings for the creation of a more complete digital archive. In the past, scholars of all kinds have deposited their materials in libraries or museums or left them with family papers. The recordings have usually been separated from academic papers and notebooks, and there has been little provision for still images, moving images and audio to be curated as a single entity. Digital technologies have, however, opened up a new set of possibilities through which a body of work can be kept together and preserved in its entirety. These technologies also offer the facility to link fieldwork recordings to contextual commentary through the creative use of metadata.

Mike O'Hanlon, Jeremy Coote and their colleagues at the Pitt Rivers Museum in Oxford have pioneered the creative online archiving of photographs and items of material culture from the southern Sudan region. The images are presented elegantly in contemporary modes of information design, and are an invaluable resource accessible to anyone with computer facilities. The Museum is also sponsoring projects that bring old ethnographic films into view along with the contexts in which they were taken—see Alison-Louise Khan's Oxford Academy of Documentary Film project, "Captured by Women". James' earliest cine footage from the 1960s is already associated with that initiative—as part of the larger project of creatively archiving her materials as a whole.

There are some striking initiatives online today, which also offer possible models for our project. There is the Sudan Open Archive of the Rift Valley Institute, for example (administered by Dan Large), focusing mainly on scarce or vulnerable written materials and the ephemeral literature of the development agencies. Visual images at present are limited to those already embedded in text as illustrations. Very different in style is the substantial and culturally focused website "Mursi Online", built around the decades-long ethnographic work of David Turton among the Mursi of south-west Ethiopia. Here we can see film clips, photos, textual descriptions and analysis, with news of ongoing development issues; and as a real innovation, the site now includes contributions from two Mursi men themselves, who visited Oxford and were able to undertake some training in making videos and maintaining the site.

Whilst our project draws on aspects of all these models, it plans to go further by inviting users to enter a world with which they can empathise despite its initial "otherness". We aim to achieve this by focusing on the conversational nature of James' recordings, to create an organised selection of materials that draws on collections contained in the archive to present a world of experiences. This world will be brought to life through sound and imagery with the fieldwork recordings speaking for themselves wherever possible. First and foremost we want the user to be able to engage directly with these recordings and for the story of James' ongoing fieldwork to unfold through this process. In order to achieve this aim, we are exploring different ways to provide contextual commentary on the recordings, to give temporal and thematic coherence to the experience without locking the user into overly didactic or linear forms of delivery.

This contextual commentary is based on short statements from James about the nature of the conversations and activities documented in her recordings, along with a series of longer reflections on her research and experiences. By including this additional material within the archive, we are building on Mikhail Bakhtin's ideas about polyphony. Bakhtin proposed that Dostoevsky's novels did not combine a "multitude of characters and fates into a single objective world, illuminated by a single authorial consciousness" but into "a plurality of consciousnesses with equal rights and each with its own world" (Bakhtin 1984: 6). Such an approach allowed for different social styles to be presented through the characters, as opposed to there being an all-pervading style dictated by the author. At the same time it also recognised the personality of the author, along with social and historical context, as being an important source of interpretation and meaning. In presenting the story of the events and changes that have occurred over the course of James' fieldwork as far as possible through the words and experiences of the people themselves, the materials will be presented in such a way as to express tensions as well as cohesion. In this sense, the point of view of the anthropologist as contextual narrator will not have final authority, with contradictory ideas and different styles of speech being able to co-exist in a more dialogic form.

Multiple windows and juxtaposition

As a means of avoiding overly didactic or linear forms of delivery, we are building on Lev Manovich's ideas about spatial montage (Manovich 2001) by using multiple windows to enable different combinations of materials to be presented on screen at any one time. Manovich argues that the computer offers a new type of cultural interface based on the aesthetics of multiple windows and graphical user interfaces. This aesthetic offers an opportunity to move away from "a logic of replacement" towards "a logic of addition and co-existence in which images can co-exist simultaneously" (ibid: 325). Unlike a book or a film, in which the structure is fixed and pre-determined, computer-based systems can be multilayered and more open-ended, enabling different pathways to be created and multiple perspectives to be explored. The key point here is for the contextual materials to be incorporated into the archive as separate data (whether it be text, audio or video), which can be placed alongside the fieldwork recordings as required without being edited in with the recordings themselves.

We are using multiple windows to present different combinations of materials to serve different purposes. For example, users might want to compare recordings across different time periods or they might want to explore a series of interlinked themes. Another possibility would be to compare recordings of actual events with interview footage of peoples' memories of these events. The materials are based on various combinations of observational recordings, interviews and informal conversations across audio, still and moving image formats. Flexibility can be built into the system to enable users to focus on a single medium or to look at them together. This comparative approach will enable the recordings to be viewed in relation to each other, to help emphasise aspects of continuity and change across time, as well as multiple points of view across a range of themes. Our aim is for this approach to help avoid the pitfalls of fossilisation, by making the system dynamic, reflexive and updatable.

The reason why we are making a distinction between the archive as a whole and the online presentation of an organised selection of James' fieldwork recordings is closely linked to ethics. Whilst on the one hand we want to provide access to the materials to as wide an audience as possible, there are constraints that go against this imperative. Although James has found that there is a strong desire amongst Uduk diaspora communities to gain access to her recordings, often this is something that they want to do in private, as the materials are politically sensitive. Some of the materials document conflict within and between communities, which is ongoing in a region where tensions persist. We therefore feel that it would not be appropriate to make the full range of the materials openly accessible as an online resource at the current time. This is an important issue on which we have begun to seek advice from related projects such as the World Oral Literature Project and the Endangered Languages Project. One solution that has been suggested is for us to consider using a password system to provide different levels of user access to the online materials (cf. Nathan, this volume).

Aston and James' strategy for the website was to focus on the less sensitive aspects of the recordings, showing the creative use of available materials such as plastic jerry cans to recreate musical traditions, and the importance of song and storytelling as a means of keeping memories alive. The organised selection of materials will extend this theme of resilience by enabling further engagement with the ways in which displaced people thrown together are able, or at least are trying, to turn their experiences into art, into fun with language, dramatic narratives, provocative enactments, witty songs, resurgent dances, and music. At the very least, they will act as a testimony to the Uduk-speaking peoples' awareness and self-knowledge of their predicament, to reveal how their deeply impassioned modes of understanding are based on conscious and ongoing reflection on their position in the world.

Our use of multiple windows is also integral to the principle of keeping the materials open to alternative interpretations both from other scholars and from the people themselves. The work at the Pitt Rivers Museum on their southern Sudan collection, for example, has led to one diaspora community re-purposing the materials for its own objectives.[1] These communities may be interested in downloading materials to incorporate into their own websites or to keep as private documents, which trigger other memories. Keeping the digital archive as a separate, but linked, entity to the online presentation will open the recordings up to alternative interpretations in the future. Additionally, by storing the contextual commentary within the archive and keeping it separate from, but linked to, the actual recordings, the option is there for this commentary to be included in these alternative interpretations.

Fluid interfaces and the communication of discrete points

In our paper for the World Oral Literature Project workshop on "Archiving Orality and Connecting with Communities"[2] (Aston and Matthews 2010), we presented work in progress as a means of illustrating our approach to developing the archive. Aston showed examples of her earlier work with James around spatial montage and fluid interfaces, with Matthews reporting on how we are applying these ideas to the development of the archive and associated online presentation.[3] A selection of Aston's examples is described below, followed by a more up-to-date summary of where we have got to in terms of scoping up our technical approach to the development of the archive and online presentation.

Through her work as a new media producer from the mid-1980s onwards and her subsequent role as a lecturer in new media production at the University of the West of England, Aston has developed her ideas around the potential of fluid interfaces and spatial montage to create new possibilities for narrative exploration. In order to create a world of experiences, with which people can empathise despite its initial "otherness", Aston has been pushing the boundaries of interface design to create flexible ways of engaging with fieldwork recordings that are poetic as opposed to informational in approach. This builds on David MacDougall's point

---

1   For example, an Anyuak group has copied material from the Pitt River's site and used it to create their own website (see Online Sources).

2   Held in December 2010 at the Centre for Research in the Arts, Social Sciences and Hunanities (CRASSH; see Online Sources).

3   This presentation was recorded and has been made available as part of the workshop documentation on the University of Cambridge Streaming Media Service (see Online Sources).

that images that directly address the senses, such as photography and film, have tended to be used within anthropological discourse as a product of language or even a language in themselves (2006: 4). In challenging this convention of making fieldwork recordings subservient to the scholarly rules of writing, Aston has been exploring ways in which the sensory nature of James' fieldwork recordings can be foregrounded to communicate specific points.

Working with the authoring tool Macromedia Director and subsequently Adobe Flash, Aston has created a series of juxtapositions that explore the application of her ideas across a range of James' fieldwork recordings. These juxtapositions were designed to create a minimum amount of clutter on the screen and encourage the user to engage intuitively with the materials. Although very similar in overall approach, there are subtle differences in the interaction techniques used, in order to explore a range of possibilities. Whilst early examples of this work have been provided elsewhere through online publication (Aston 2010), more examples are provided here, to illustrate how they are feeding into the current phase of development.[4] There are six examples in total, with the last two containing additional contextual analysis in the form of audio narration provided by James. All of these clips were recorded by James unless otherwise indicated. Screenshots from these six videos are presented below; please see Online Sources for the web addresses of the full video clips.

The first example shows three video clips placed side by side, to illustrate a point made in one of James' published papers about different ways in which the Uduk people remember traumatic events (James 1997). In the first of these clips, taken from the rushes of the Granada film (Macdonald 1993), we see Martha Ahmed[5] in a transit refugee camp at Karmi talking in a very matter-of-fact way about the recent shooting of her sister's teenage son. This was a relatively recent incident and her report is very graphic. In the second clip, from Bonga 1994, we see Peke Shigwami[6] reflecting on the disappearance of her daughter, who has been missing for several years. The anxiety that she is suffering is very evident in her interactions with James.

---

4   Whilst the paper in the Forum of Qualitative Social Research (Aston 2010) provides interactive examples authored in Flash, in the name of widening accessibility, we have attached video screen-casts of these examples to this chapter, via a series of online links.

5   One of the key refugee women's leaders, who had some years of schooling before the war. She has subsequently become a member of the Blue Nile state assembly.

6   Her daughter married a rebel soldier in the first refugee camp. He took her off in a different direction when people suddenly had to flee from a later camp.

In the third clip, also taken in Bonga 1994, we see Nathaniel Gurempa[7] using storytelling to remind people of a moment of hysteria in which a group of Uduk had a vision of angels taking them back to their homeland. This was an event that happened a while ago, which can now be recounted as a story, to the evident amusement of his audience.

A fluid interface enables users to move between these clips at their own pace and in an intuitive way, to enable close investigation with the materials in ways that would not be possible within a sequentially-edited film. In addition to this, the different use of language across the three clips, along with the layers of non-verbal communication contained within them, create a much richer description than could be achieved through words alone. The user can click to focus in on a single clip and view subtitles as Martha, Peke or Nathaniel speak. If the user goes back to the three clips interface, the video carries on where he/she left off, making the experience more engaging than with more standard forms of a point and click interface.[8]

Figure 1.   Screenshot of "Three Ways of Remembering". Image by Judith Aston and Paul Matthews, 2012.

7   Like Martha, he was educated at the old mission school and is a staunch member of the church community.

8   Such approaches in which the video carries on where the user left off are rapidly becoming more commonplace, as the use of online video grows in sophistication. A good example is the facility to move fluidly between small and full-screen video on sites like YouTube, the difference here being in the employment of these interfaces within a multiple windows environment.

The second example shows how a single clip, such as the one of Martha talking about the shooting of her nephew, can be analysed in more detail, by placing the written transcription alongside the clip. The user can go to different sections of the clip by clicking on the corresponding section of the written transcription. In so doing, a detailed analysis of the relationship between the spoken word and the non-verbal communication that surrounds it can be made, in a way that is unique to computer-based multimedia interfaces. It was this potential to link written transcriptions to the actual recording from which they are taken that first attracted James to working with Aston and which has led to the current collaboration. From her earlier experience of acting as a consultant to the "Disappearing World" film on the Uduk (Macdonald 1993), James has written that "a film can record the facial and body expression of listeners as well as speakers; and the memory of 'fear' can be invoked even when it is not actually named by anybody" (James 1997). However, her frustration with filmmaking is that clips such as this become embedded within the structure of a sequentially edited narrative, thus limiting the possibility for in-depth analysis of individual recordings.

Figure 2.   Screenshot of a single clip analysis. Image by Judith Aston and
Paul Matthews, 2012.

In the third example, the same clip of Martha is juxtaposed alongside a clip of the journey of displacement to which she is referring. This clip is of a piece of footage recorded by a French news crew in a temporary refugee camp in Itang 1990, in which Martha shows them the terrible conditions under which her people are struggling to survive. The user can watch each of these clips in turn or move between them at will, focusing in on a single clip as appropriate. Whilst toggling between full-screen and small-screen presentation of video clips is now standard practice on the Internet, the difference here is the facility provided for the simultaneous presentation of clips within a fluid interface environment. In this case, it enables recollections of past experiences and events to be presented alongside actual footage of those experiences and events.

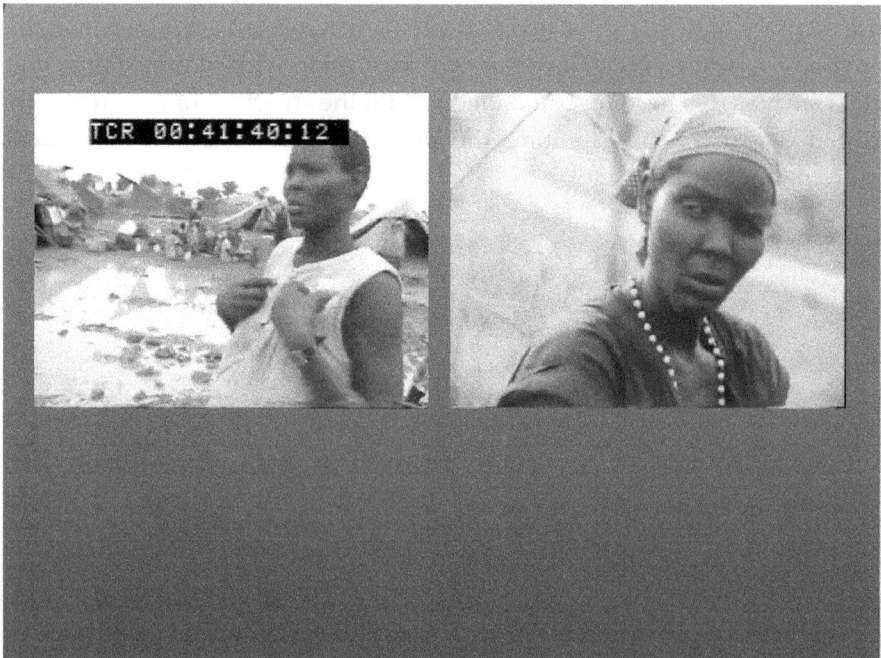

Figure 3.   Screenshot from video showing events and memories. Image by Judith Aston and Paul Matthews, 2012.

Multiple windows can also be used to make visual resonances across time, as seen in this next example in which cine recordings from village hamlets in the 1960s are compared with Hi-8 video recordings taken in the semi-permanent refugee camp in Bonga, Ethiopia in 1994 and 2000. The comparisons have been carefully selected to show how certain aspects of rural village life were being recreated in the camp, at a time of relative stability compared to the previous traumas of constant displacement. Observational footage of everyday activities, such as making coffee, drinking beer, preparing grinding stones and playing music, are juxtaposed to show aspects of continuity and change across the two time periods. In the interactive version, the user can move fluidly between looking at each clip individually or making comparisons across time through on-screen juxtaposition. This video demonstrator, however, focuses in on the juxtapositions as a more direct way of making the point through linear video.

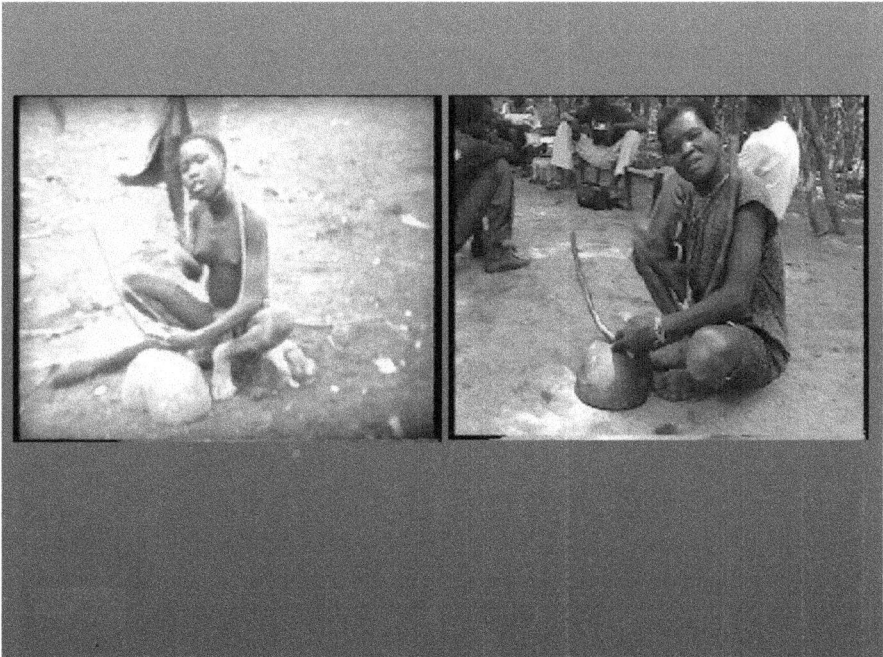

Figure 4.   Screenshot of comparisons across time. Image by Judith Aston and Paul Matthews, 2012.

This next example juxtaposes three video clips also recorded in Bonga: a mother and child preparing a grinding stone; two women working together; and a further clip of two groups of women performing the same activity. The clips can be played simultaneously or one at a time, via a simple keyboard command. Another keyboard command brings up an audio recording of James talking about the three clips and how the sound that they are making is very evocative of village life in the 1960s. She explains how there is a playfulness to the rhythms and sounds that are being created that is rich in meaning and resonance, both for her and for the Uduk people themselves. This audio narration can be turned on and off at will, always continuing where it left off, with the clips themselves conveying this sense of playfulness.

Figure 5.   Screenshot of evocative soundscapes. Image by Judith Aston and
Paul Matthews, 2012.

The final example combines cine footage from the 1960s of the diviners' dance with accompanying reel-to-reel audio. This material is then juxtaposed alongside video footage from the refugee camp, in which William Danga[9] produces from his hut a copy of The Listening Ebony (James 1999).[10] A crowd soon gathers round as he starts to look at the photographs inside it and to reminisce on the events that they document. The juxtaposition provides a very suggestive link between past images and sounds and their current value, as the pictures that

---

9   One of James' old friends from the 1960s.

10   James had given this book as a replacement for the one she had given years previously but which had not survived the most recent journeys.

they are looking at are also of the diviners' dance. This link is made explicit via James' audio commentary, in which she explains that she was deliberately aiming to capture the reflexivity of them looking at these photographs, whilst she was making a video recording of them doing this. The multimedia presentation adds yet another layer to this, opening up further possibilities for reflexive engagement with James' fieldwork recordings.

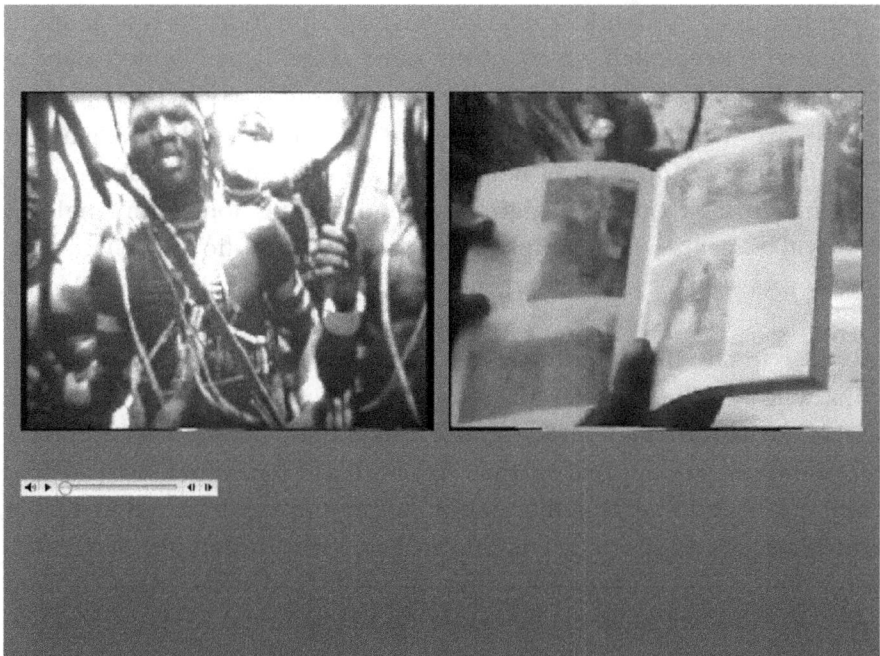

Figure 6.   Screenshot of reflexive juxtaposition. Image by Judith Aston and Paul Matthews, 2012.

Incorporating fluid interfaces into the current phase of development

The prior development of these demonstrator interfaces has inspired the technical approach that we have taken to the current phase of the project. It has been our basis for looking at how the archive might be organised and how metadata might enable this type of interaction more flexibly through the interface. A key concern of our current work, therefore, is to establish working methods that tackle the combined requirements of curation, archiving and the creation of exploratory interfaces.

We have found that James' recordings can be quite thoroughly described using an organisation that encompasses the area of recording and the time (corresponding to research visits to the Sudan and to diaspora communities in the USA). Category and hierarchy need to then be divided and expanded into broader themes, more detailed keywords and specific people and events. One key requirement is to incorporate two kinds of semantics: those relating to the primary content of the media, and those relating to the subject of the conversation or focus of the activity portrayed. This is in order to extend our work around reflexive juxtaposition, such as an event paired with people talking about the same event. It will be necessary to distinguish between these two types at times, whilst linking them at others.

We are working with a colleague at the Oxford Academy of Documentary Film, who is helping James with the basic digitisation, logging and cataloguing. Logging of video is being done with Final Cut Pro, with clips then being imported together with audio and still images into the desktop media asset management system Expression Media. This enables metadata to be exported as XML and then transformed in order to structure the interface. Additional segmentation for video clips will be achieved using a tool such as Frameline47, with subclip metadata exported to MPEG-7 and integrated. In terms of interface technologies, we appreciate that Adobe Flash remains a very useful front-end technology for the manipulation and combination of media, and is widely supported. For this reason early prototypes were built using Flash with dynamic loading of media and metadata files from XML. At the same time we are exploring the potential of HTML5 native video to support the kinds of interaction we have envisaged with a view to longer term sustainability.

We have also been encouraged by the work of the Pad.ma project, a standards-based web platform for sharing ethnographic video accompanied by metadata and commentary. The Pad.ma tools let you look at video clips and scan through them, look at the whole object data and then go through to looking at timeline data. This is the type of interface that will allow the sharing and layering of metadata by different individuals over the web. Here we have applied these tools to the clip of Martha talking about her nephew to illustrate how it works.

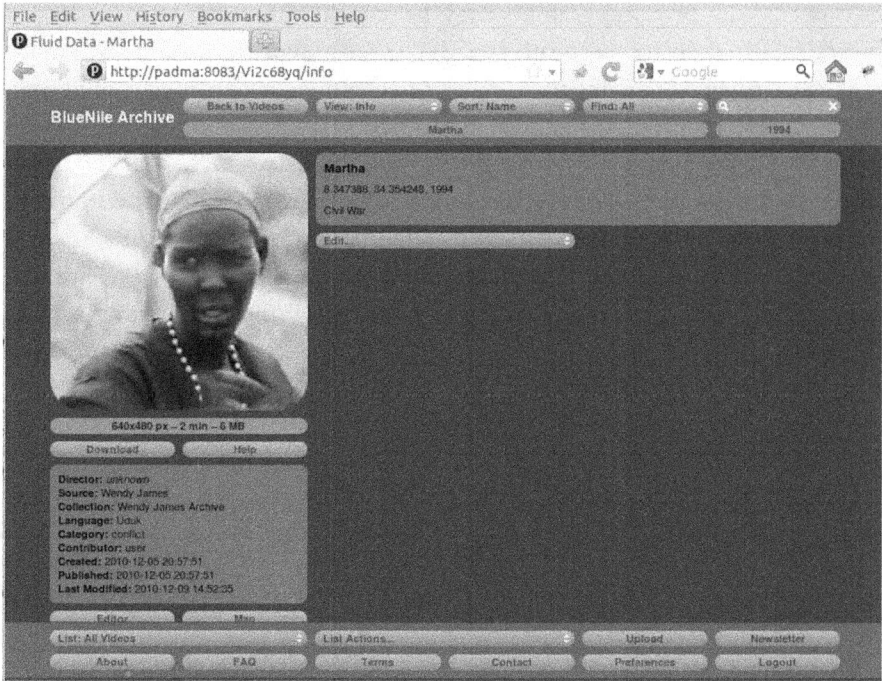

Figure 7.   Screenshot of Pad.ma prototype. Image by Judith Aston and Paul Matthews, 2012.

An outline architecture of the prototype system is shown below. The media catalogue is exported as XML, which is then transformed into a simplified subset of metadata as JSON (JavaScript Object Notation). This in turn is brought into the web application where filtering and clustering can be achieved using JavaScript. Thumbnails initially represent the media objects, which are then enlarged when the user selects items of interest.

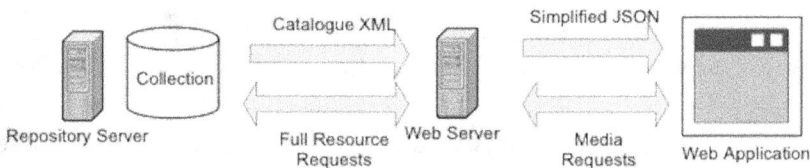

Figure 8.   Architecture of fluid data prototype. Image by Judith Aston and Paul Matthews, 2010.

In our HTML5 prototype, items may be selected according to theme and period/place, then brought into a media browser, which presents two main videos or images. A k-means cluster of resources according to metadata (with a set of binaries for each item reflecting inclusion or exclusion in a metadata term) results in the ability to juxtapose resources on the same theme by time and place. In this example, the selection of items within the music and dance theme collects two of James' slides from the 1960s taken among the neighbouring Gumuz people just inside Ethiopia. They show a girl making music with holes in the ground at the start of the rainy season. The slides are accompanied by sound and video narration to provide further context and an immersive experience.

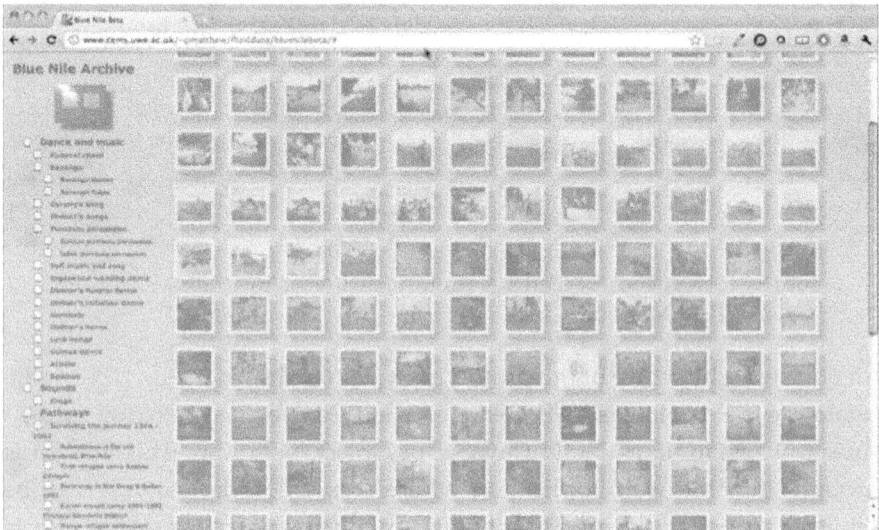

Figure 9.   Screenshot of HTML5 prototype. Image by Judith Aston
Paul Matthews, 2012.

We have begun incorporating narrative video fragments applied to specific recordings and to comparative clusters, which are based on themes. The next phase of work will seek to provide longer introductions to James' intermittent engagement with the Uduk since the mid-1960s. These introductions will reveal the changing nature of her fieldwork over time and introduce reflexivity into the presentation of her materials. With metadata linking illustrative media to these longer narrations, the intention is to then provide a coherent guided trail through the material that the user may choose to sample or follow at length. We have successfully piloted the recording of narrative using a webcam while the collection is being viewed; this approach can also be taken with other commentators.

This chapter has demonstrated our prototypes and working methods for the development of an end-to-end system for the archiving and future exploration of an important ethnographic collection. As such, we are addressing the need for collections such as these to be humanised: for additional layers of meaning to be applied. We have also shown how metadata, carried through from the repository level, can be used to underpin media montage at the interface, with potential for the discovery of spatial and temporal contrasts and resonances. In mapping Aston's ideas around fluid interfaces and narrative exploration onto Matthew's knowledge of database systems and archive workflow processes, we are aiming to immerse our users in a world of experiences, through which they will gain insights into James' fieldwork and into the impact of civil war on a marginal community.

We want this world of experiences to foreground the fact that many of James' recordings are based on informal conversations at different historical periods, between the anthropologist and her informants and amongst the informants themselves. Through revealing the ongoing nature of these conversations and linking them to observational footage of everyday life and events, our aim is to remain true to the fluidity of oral tradition over time and to avoid fossilisation. This is why we have begun to record James' thoughts and memories, as evoked by her engaging with the prototypes that we have been developing. In the same way that many of her recordings in the field are based on intermittent and ongoing conversations, we are aiming for her commentary to have a similar feel and to be grounded in an oral as opposed to literary tradition.

While we are fully aware that this is an ambitious project and that compromises will inevitably have to be made to create a coherent final product, we hope that its outcomes will go some way towards doing justice to James' work and to fostering empathy with the people whose memories, hopes and enthusiasms are conveyed within her recordings. We also hope that this work will find resonance both within and beyond the academy, to increase understanding around the predicament of a marginal community struggling to make its way in the modern world. Finally, we hope that the approaches and suggestions offered here will provide inspiration to others working in related areas, whether as academic fieldworkers, community activists or interested bystanders.

References

Aston, Judith, 'Spatial Montage and Multimedia Ethnography: Using Computers to Visualise Aspects of Migration and Social Division Among a Displaced Community', *Forum: Qualitative Social Research*, 11:2 (2010) <http://www.qualitative-research.net/index.php/fqs/article/view/1479> [Accessed 24 October 2012].

—, and Paul Matthews, 'Co-creation and Multiple Curation: Making an Archive Relevant to Contemporary Contexts', paper presented at the workshop *Archiving Orality and Connecting with Communities*, (Cambridge: World Oral Literature Project, 2010) filmed and presented online: <http://sms.cam.ac.uk/media/1092085> [Accessed 24 October 2012].

Bakhtin, Mikhail, *Problems of Dostoevsky's Poetics*, ed. and trans. by Caryl Emerson (Manchester: University of Manchester Press, 1984) Orig. Russian ed. 1929.

James, Wendy, *The Listening Ebony: Moral Knowledge, Religion and Power among the Uduk of Sudan* (Oxford: Clarendon Press, 1988). Paperback ed. with new Preface, 1999.

—, 'The Names of Fear: History, Memory and the Ethnography of Feeling among Uduk Refugees', *Journal Royal Anthropological Institute N.S*, 3 (1997), 115–131.

MacDougall, David, *The Corporeal Image: Film, Ethnography and the Senses* (New Jersey: Princetown University Press, 2006).

Manovich, Lev, *The Language of New Media* (Cambridge, MA: MIT Press, 2001).

Films/videos

MacDonald, Bruce, dir., *Orphans of Passage*, Disappearing World (Granada TV, broadcast 18 May 1993).

Online Sources

Anyuak group website, with material from the Pitt Rivers website <http://www.anyuakmedia.com/Anyuak%20Mini%20Museum/index.htm>

Judith Aston and Paul Matthews, video of presentation made at World Oral Literature Project's 2010 workshop, *Multiple Audiences and Co-curation: Linking an Ethnographic Archive to Contemporary Contexts* <http://sms.cam.ac.uk/media/1092085>

Judith Aston and Wendy James (2007), *Voices from the Blue Nile* <http://www.voicesfromthebluenile.org>

Judith Aston, Wendy James and Paul Matthews (2012), *Voices from the Blue Nile, Clip 1: "Three Ways of Remembering"* <http://www.voicesfromthebluenile.org/wolp/1>

Judith Aston, Wendy James and Paul Matthews (2012), *Voices from the Blue Nile, Clip 2: single clip analysis* <http://www.voicesfromthebluenile.org/wolp/2>

Judith Aston, Wendy James and Paul Matthews (2012), *Voices from the Blue Nile,*
    Clip 3: video showing events and memories
    <http://www.voicesfromthebluenile.org/wolp/3>

Judith Aston, Wendy James and Paul Matthews (2012), *Voices from the Blue Nile,*
    clip 4: comparisons across time
    <http://www.voicesfromthebluenile.org/wolp/4>

Judith Aston, Wendy James and Paul Matthews (2012), *Voices from the Blue Nile,*
    clip 5: Screenshot of evocative soundscapes
    <http://www.voicesfromthebluenile.org/wolp/5>

Judith Aston, Wendy James and Paul Matthews (2012), *Voices from the Blue Nile,*
    clip 6: reflexive juxtaposition
    <http://www.voicesfromthebluenile.org/wolp/6>

Judith Aston, Wendy James and Paul Matthews (2012), *Voices from the Blue Nile,*
    clip 7: Pad.ma prototype
    <http://www.voicesfromthebluenile.org/wolp/7>

Judith Aston, Wendy James and Paul Matthews (2012), *Voices from the Blue Nile,*
    clip 8: HTML5 prototype
    <http://www.voicesfromthebluenile.org/wolp/8>

Final Cut Pro
    <http://www.apple.com/finalcutpro>

Frameline TV
    <http://www.frameline.tv/>

Hans Rausing Endangered Languages Project
    <http://www.hrelp.org/>

Mursi Online
    <http://www.mursi.org>

Now Media Pro
    <http://www.phaseone.com/en/Imaging-Software/Media-Pro.aspx>

Mike O'Hanlon, Jeremy Coote and the Pitt Rivers Museum, Oxford, *Sudan Open*
    Archive
    <http://www.sudanarchive.net>

Oxford Academy of Documentary Film, *Captured by Women*
    <http://www.oadf.co.uk/blog/category/captured-by-women/>

Pad.ma
    <http://pad.ma/>

Pitt Rivers Museum on Sudan
    <http://southernsudan.prm.ox.ac.uk>

World Oral Literature Project
    <http://www.oralliterature.org/>

World Oral Literature Project, December 2010 workshop, held at the Centre for
    Research in the Arts, Social Sciences and Humanities, Cambridge
    <http://www.crassh.cam.ac.uk/events/1327>

II. Engagements and Reflections from the Field

4. Researchers as Griots? Reflections on Multimedia Fieldwork in West Africa

Daniela Merolla and Felix Ameka, in collaboration with Kofi Dorvlo

In the beginning

Daniela Merolla and Kofi Dorvlo started a video documentation project in 2007 on Ewe migration stories and the festival in which these stories are re-enacted, *Hogebetsotso*. Oral sources and archaeological remains suggest that a series of migrations started in the eleventh century and that Ewes settled in Ghana in the early seventeenth century.[1] Oral narratives called *xotutu* recount a flow of people from the town called Notsie (in central Togo) to Ghana. The departure from Notsie is enacted in the *Hogebetsotso* festival ("leaving Hogbe", i.e. leaving the ancestral land) that takes place in several Anlo towns in Ghana. Merolla and Dorvlo's project aimed to investigate what the festival contributes to the discourse of the migration tradition, whether there are other local versions recounted orally and what the present written/oral/new media interactions are.[2] The project

---

1 The contemporary Ewe settlements span from the bank of the Mono River at the Togo-Benin border to Ghana, where large Ewe communities live along the eastern side of the Volta Lake, and in the area around Keta Lagoon on the seacoast (Amenumey 1997; Gayibor and Aguigah 2005).

2 The performance is an artistic, cultural and social event that constructs meanings and networks including but also going beyond the uttered words. What gets lost in the written transcription are the intonation and gestures along with the eventual

DOI: 10.111647/OBP.0032..05

also envisaged collecting video materials of the Ewe migration stories during the festival in the framework of the Verba Africana series.[3] The *Hogbetsotso* festival is usually held in the first week of November every year. Merolla and Dorvlo had hoped to be participant observers and documenters during the 2007 festival. However, in that year and ever since, the festival has not been held due to disputes surrounding the chieftaincy of the Anlo paramountcy.[4] In November 2007, given the volatile situation in Anloga, Merolla and Dorvlo were not able to visit the area, instead we interviewed Datey-Kumodzie[5] who had been recommended to us as being well informed about the *Hogebetsotso* festival and the migration stories. The interview was different from what we had expected.

At the beginning of November 2009, Felix Ameka, Merolla and Dorvlo were together in Accra, and watched and discussed the interview before

---

musical accompaniment, the interactions between performer and public, the clothing and scenography, and the context and politics of the performance (Barber 1997; Coulet Western 1975; Baumgardt and Bounfour 2000; Furniss 1996; Görög-Karady 1981; Finnegan 1992; Okpewho 1992; Ricard and Veit-Wild 2005; Schipper 1990). The necessity of new media in documentation and research is strengthened by the changing conditions of oral production in the last decade, for instance on the Internet (Merolla 2002 and 2005). However, while video captures much more than text and sound, it also has limitations with respect to some aspects of the context of performance: the smell, for example. Moreover, the case presented in these pages shows that technology can effect change in what is recorded.

3   The Verba Africana series produces DVDs and CD-Roms for libraries and is freely accessible on the Internet (see Online Sources). It was started by Merolla thanks to the collaboration between Leiden and Naples Universities in 2005. Verba Africana was integrated into the international project "African Oral literatures, new media and technologies" (coordinated by Merolla and Jan Jansen) supported by INALCO (Paris), SOAS (London), the Universities of Hamburg, Leiden, and Naples, the Netherlands Organization for Scientific Research and since 2010 by the World Oral Literature Project (Cambridge, UK), the Language Centre of the University of Ghana (Accra, Ghana), the School of Languages of Rhodes University (South Africa), and the University of Bamako (Mali). For information on the project see Online Sources for the Leiden University site. The series is open to all Africanist scholars. The idea underlying the Verba Africana series is that textual content and visual performance are both essential for classification, description and interpretation of the oral genres and their narrative context. The performance of African oral genres, whether classic poems, songs and tales or innovative genres such as hip hop and AIDS theatre, is recorded and integrated to allow the interested public to approach oral literary productions as total events distributed in several layers: video fragments and summaries on the menu, with the possibility to view accompanying material on subpages. Accompanying material includes background information, excerpts of studies and articles, interviews, transcription, translation, presentation and analysis of the context and of visual aspects of the performance.

4   In February 2011, the dispute was resolved and a new Paramount Chief was installed. It is hoped that the celebrations will resume again in November 2011.

5   Dr. Datey-Kumodzie does not use his first name (Samuel) in his recent publications.

Dorvlo and Merolla went on fieldwork to the Anlo area. Merolla and Dorvlo went to carry out their initial research project and made a series of recordings and interviews at Anloga, the capital town of the Anlo area in Ghana, and the centre of the *Hogebetsotso* festival. Among other aspects, they investigated what people thought of the stories and interpretations offered during the first interview. In this case also, some of the answers differed from what we expected. We return to this point below when discussing the relationship between personal and shared cultural knowledge.

Xotutu narratives and the making of the *Hogbetsotso* festival

The Ewe exodus was probably caused by the progressive expansion of other populations, most likely the Yoruba (Amenumey 1997: 15–16; Gayibor and Aguigah 2005: 6–7). Several *xotutu* versions agree that the Ewe moved westward from northern areas in present-day Benin and settled, following successive displacements and subdivisions, in what is nowadays Togo and eastern Ghana. Through genealogies of royal characters, narratives of migrations collected at Tado (along the Mono River) relate that Adja and Ewe peoples came from Ketu in Yoruba country, while narratives collected at Notsie recount another flow of migration from Tado to Notsie. The most frequently narrated story includes the migration from Notsie to Ghana during the reign of Agokoli I, a cruel king who asked the Ewes (then called Dogbos) to kill their elders, to build houses and the city wall with mud and pieces of glass, rock and thorns and to produce "a rope out of clay". The Ewes were able to escape from Notsie thanks to a cunning trick: they left the town walking backwards so that nobody could guess from the direction of their footsteps that they were leaving. In such narratives, Notsie is presented as the Ewe ancestral home. Some versions collected in Anlo-Ewe include the episode of the conflict between Agokoli and Sri, chief of the Dogbos in Notsie, which fuelled Agokoli's harsh behaviour towards the Dogbos/Ewes. Other stories narrate incidents that took place after the Ewe departed from Notsie, such as the episode relating how the right to alternate succession to the Anlo stool (symbol of ritual and political authority) was established between the Bate clan and the Adzovia clan (Aduamah 1965: 5–6, 18–20).

The theme of inter-generational conflict, whether between king and elders or between father and son, is widely encountered in West African oral narratives (Paulme 1976: 91–121; Görög-Karady 1995). Similarly, the motif of the "rope of clay" is common in West African and Arabic narratives (Gayibor 1984: 31; Pazzi 1973: 24). In the Notsie narrative such themes are specified and localised. As indicated above, there is an episode in the narrative where the king Agokoli orders the elders to be killed. This episode highlights the political conflict between kingship and *amega* (council of elders) in a system in which the spiritual and political leader was usually secluded from public view and the council was the political power that communicated with the people.

> A young foolish Agokoli seeks to rid himself of the confining advice of his elders by ordering all to be executed. His Ewe subjects, however, are successful in saving a few from death [...] And it is the elders who successfully lead them [the Ewe] out of Notsie when they make their escape. (Greene 2002a: 1035)

If the solution offered in the Notsie narrative re-states the authority of the elders, other stories offer a more ambiguous discourse on seniority. For example, a version collected by Gayibor (1984: 27) recounts that one of the elders became drunk during a celebration and revealed the trick played by Ewe people to induce Agokoli to kill his own son; a revelation that gave sway to the retaliation of Agokoli and the order to kill the elders. According to Sandra Greene, the theme of elderly authority gained particular importance when social, political and economic changes during colonialism jeopardised the social system based on seniority, "Resistance to this change in the authority culture of the area took a number of forms, but perhaps the most interesting was the popularity of narratives that reinforced elderly authority" (2002: 1034).

An intense interaction between oral and written *xotutu* versions has taken place since the colonial period. According to Gayibor (1989) and Greene (2002a), the German missionaries who were active in the area since 1847 promoted not only linguistic standardisation based on the Anlo-Ewe language, but also the idea of a common origin of all Ewes from the city of Notsie. The *xotutu* versions identifying Notsie as the "original home" were known in the Anlo area (present south-eastern Ghana) and became generally accepted since they were used for the reconstruction of Ewe migratory displacements in the missionary school readers.[6]

---

6   The Ghanaian priest Henry Kwakume offered one of the first full-length versions of the migration story in French translation (1948).

Ces traditions, lues à travers tout le pays ewe à la fin du siècle dernier et au début de celui-ci [1900] ont fini par s'enraciner solidement dans le cœur et l'esprit de ces jeunes élèves [...] Les jeunes écoliers d'hier sont devenus les veillards qui, de nos jours, nous répètent avec conviction ce que les missionaires leur avaient patiemment appris.

[These traditions read throughout Eweland toward the end of the last century and the beginning of this century (1900) have firmly taken root in the hearts and minds of the pupils [...] the pupils of yesterday became the elders who in our days repeat with conviction what they were patiently taught by the missionaries].[7] (Gayibor 1989: 212; translated by Merolla and Ameka)

The belief that Notsie was the "original home" of the Ewe was further strengthened by both political and religious movements (Gayibor 1989: 212; Greene 2002a: 1035). The Ewe (pre-independence) nationalist movements referred to their common origin when they sought to include all Ewe-speaking peoples into one of the nations to be created after the end of European colonisation. An important moment for the diffusion of such views was the rally organised at Notsie in 1956, on the occasion of the first *Agbogbo* (referring to Notsie's wall) festival, when the authorities—reunited from all the Ewe-speaking areas—decided to harmonise their historical narratives.[8] On the other hand, following Greene:

The Notsie narrative's popularity was further enhanced during the colonial period among the ordinary and the average in the religion as a result of local efforts to make sense of their own traditions in light of the Biblical narratives introduced by the Bremen Mission. Instead of embracing the notion that they were the children of Ham who had diverted from the path of God and who needed the guiding hand of the missionaries to lead them back onto the road of righteousness, many among the Ewe associated their exodus from Notsie with the Jews' escape from Egypt. The Ewes were not heathens but had been one with the Israelites.[9] (2002a: 1035–36)

---

7   See, for example, the missionary school reader by Hartter, Spieth and Daeuble (1906).

8   "A cette occasion, tous les chefs réunis confrontèrent leurs traditions [ ] De là naquit également la tendance à uniformisation des récits historiques des differents chefs en ce qui concerne les phases de l'histoire antérieure à la dispersion de Notsie" [On this occasion, all the assembled chiefs confronted their traditions [...] From there was born the trend to standardise the historical accounts of the various leaders concerning the history prior to the dispersion from Notsie] (Gayibor 1989: 212; translated by Merolla and Ameka).

9   Greene mentions a number of authors who favoured this interpretation, such as Mamattah (1979) and Fianu (1986).

All these narratives of migration, whether orally transmitted or written down, give form to and convey knowledge of the Ewe land and community, crystallising historical processes of identification through migrations, settlements, interactions with, and interpretations by different groups. An example is the re-enactment of the migration journey in the *Hogbetsotso* festival.

The departure from Notsie is indeed enacted in the *Hogbetsotso* festival that takes place in several Anlo-Ewe (Aŋlɔ in Ewe orthography) towns such as Anloga, Anyako, Dzodze and Klikor in Ghana (Nukunya 1997: 106; Anyidoho 2005: 4). *Hogbetsotso* is a recent phenomenon, as it was created in the 1960s.[10] At the beginning, storytelling was included as part of the festival but in the 1980s the organisation chose for a dramatic form, as indicated by Greene:

> In 1978 […] a clan elder who was widely respected for his knowledge of the oral history of the area, presented a most dignified and moving account of Notsie's history and the exodus that mesmerized those who attended. The audience was sparse, however, and over the years it attracted even fewer interested observers […] Refusing to abandon the very heart of the festival, the organizers had opted by 1996 to pursue another approach. That year, they invited a drama troupe from Accra to perform the exodus re-enactment. The response was overwhelming […]. Significantly, to attract such a crowd, the troupe took considerable artistic license in dramatizing the events leading to the exodus. Agokoli was portrayed not as the insensitive tyrant of the well-known Notsie narrative, but in slapstick form as a drunken, lecherous, bumbling ruler who was presented as more an object of amusement than abhorrence. The fact that only a more light-hearted account […] could draw such an engaged crowd illustrates the extent to which older meanings and memories have undergone yet another set of transformations. (2002b: 27–28)

The power of the Ewe migration narratives as a means to negotiate and create identity is still perceptible in the present, as illustrated by the video interview discussed in this paper, integrating them in the eclectic combination of different forms of knowledge in the contemporary globalised world.

---

10   In 1962, Anlo developed what became an annual festival commemorating the exodus from Notsie. Named Hogbetsotsoza (from the Ewe words hogbe [homeland], understood to be Notsie; tsotso [exodus therefrom]; and za [festival], the organisers used this particular title because Notsie (or Hogbe) was known to every Anlo who had either been taught or had heard about the history of the Ewes in school or from local traditions. In the first year of its organisation and in all those festivals held since, however, emphasis was placed not on a larger Ewe cultural identity, but rather on identifying and taking pride in Anlo culture (Greene 2002b: 26).

The interview with Datey-Kumodzie

The meeting started with a preliminary exchange on the aims and the publication of the interview. The interviewee explained at the beginning that he obtained his doctorate in Germany on Ewe sacred songs and that indeed he was involved in and knowledgeable about the *Hogebetsotso* festival and the migration stories as he was academically and personally engaged in the religious and philosophical Ewe world of cults and shrines.[11] We asked the interviewee whether he knew what kind of Ewe migration stories were narrated orally and their role and meaning in the organisation and functioning of the *Hogebetsotso* festival. He made it clear that he was the repository of a very special, secret knowledge that no other researcher could reveal and that he was worried about "people tapping and stealing" his knowledge. He then added that he needed to be careful because it was explosive ("volatile") knowledge about the distorted history of the Ewes and how such distortions contributed to destroying the continent of Africa. He told us that he had sent his book on this subject to UNESCO but they had refused to publish it because "they became afraid". We confirmed that we would publish the interview with his name and that the aim of our project was to create materials for research and teaching that were to be distributed through university libraries. As at the beginning he had mentioned that there was much more involved than the migration stories alone, we took his hint and asked whether he would tell us about that too.

At this point he started to explain the meaning of the term *Hogebetsotso*, framing it in a cosmological geography of the Ewe areas of origin and their present location that he presented as not generally known because people would have forgotten the meaning of their language. He also described the kind of dance that re-enacts the central episode of the migration story (the Ewe walking backward from Notsie), interpreting it in a metaphorical and philosophical way. Then he started to sing, using his song to link the origin of the Ewe to the creation of the world by the Mother Goddess. From this point on, with a powerful performance in terms of singing and narrating style, he recounted that human beings had crept out of water after centuries of evolution, "they were dolphins". The first migration

---

11 Datey-Kumodzie is committed to the Hu-Yaweh cult that is related to the neo-traditionalist religious mission Afrikania (De Witte 2008: 135). He introduced himself as the president of the Sophia Mission during the interview. Datey-Kumodzie's dissertation was defended in 1989.

started from the Lost Continent of Mu from which the original Ewe speakers spread to the whole world, to India and China, to Mesopotamia, to the ancient Greco-Roman world and Egypt. From Ethiopia, the ancient Ewes migrated to Egypt and from there they went south towards Nigeria. From that point on, his narratives reconnected to the known oral migration stories of the Ewes. However, he added another wave of migration from west to east from ancient Ghana down through present day Gonja, Ashanti and Ga territories before crossing the Volta eastwards to the Anlo area. He claimed that this was the route his family had followed.[12]

During his performance, he repeatedly used etymologies and linguistic connections as evidence for his narrative. He had his story ready and well developed, and we did not need to ask questions to go on. In fact, only a few times did Merolla try to re-address the initial question on the role of the migration narratives in the *Hogebetsotso* (and whether the songs he sang were used during the *Hogebetsotso*) and he did return to it at the end of the interview. As a whole, he executed an impressive performance, alternating between narrative and song.

The interview can be approached from myriad angles. As a performance, it was very rich in gestures, for example, the flowing movement accompanying the narration of the first human beings emerging from water. Overall, the connection of gestures to narrative style is extremely effective and beautiful. We will focus, however, on the content and its impact in relation to the "invention of tradition" argument and the interviewee/researcher relationship in terms of the transmission of knowledge and the possible influence of such narratives in society when diffused through educational channels, as it happened in previous times when missionaries spread their version of Ewe migration stories.

An attempt at interpretation

As explained, the expectation was to interview a scholar narrating and explaining various versions of the Ewe migration story, the development of the *Hogebetsotso* festival, and the interpretation of the narratives in symbolic and philosophical terms.

---

12   If this is true, it would mean that his family are not "true" Anlo and that they might be called dzideéhlɔme "born into the clan".

Contrary to expectations, the scholar's narrative appears to be a convoluted mix of Ewe cosmological ideas, migration stories, scientific ideas on evolution, historical knowledge of different periods and cultures, and popularising fictional narratives of the Lost Continent of Mu. Moreover, the interviewee's narrative was "Ewe-centric" in so far as the language spoken by the first human beings was Ewe and this language and cosmological knowledge fertilised and left traces in the best known civilisations of the whole world.

Let it be stated clearly that the problem with this interview is not in the mixing of heterogeneous materials or in its ethnocentricity. It is well known that narrative strategies and what is sometimes called the mythopoetic approach make it possible for storytellers to integrate different forms of knowledge from varied sources alongside input from the audience and adapt them to present circumstances. The interviewee's narrative can be read in line with the discussion on the constant process of identity formation and the making of tradition. Linking one's ancestors to major civilisations is a feature of the identity (re)construction and is a response as well to a variety of cultural predicaments, such as political and ideological discussions around nationalism and pan-Africanism, globalising processes in knowledge building, and the need to find/re-state one's location in the mental geography and history that stretch to include the whole world. We also see the linking of ancestors to major civilisations as a brave attempt to find a role for local knowledge—but in a learned and esoteric elaboration—that cannot just be put "aside" because it risks becoming ineffective and futile when segregated in the realm of mythology or philosophy.

Questions and problems

In making the Verba Africana volume on Ewe migration narratives it was decided to include only the less controversial parts of the interview, and present them as video fragments. Problematic parts of the interview are, however, presented in written form accompanying the video. As indicated before, although the problems connected to the selection are linked to the characteristics of the Verba Africana series that address researchers as well as students and the interested public, our experience is connected to the discussion on the theory and methodology of video fieldwork and documentation.

The first issue encountered was that the interviewee is and presents himself as a researcher, and his position urges us to consider the scientific value of his narrative and whether he is in search of legitimisation, as the initial story of UNESCO's refusal to publish his book seems to suggest.

The ethical and scientific knot is that we intend to publish a video interview that respects the original discourse of the interviewee but at the same time we do not want to be incorporated into his personal agenda by endorsing his complex narrative as scientific, nor do we intend to publicise his agenda or spread it as history among Ewe, Ghanaian and international students and among Ewe people. We wish to avoid falling into the same trap that missionary discourses, through their teaching and preaching, have generated among the Ewe. Last but not least, we are confronted with the interviewee's role and ambition in present day Ghanaian and Ewe society. He presents himself as a pillar, leader and mover of a "Sophia movement"[13] that seeks to revitalise local religious knowledge and to make it accessible for a larger audience; possibly as a viable alternative to Christianity and Islam.[14]

Our scientific problems

Etymologies

In the interview, etymologies are offered as evidence to sustain an elaborate narrative that mingles mythological creation stories, "scientific" evolutionism, popularising narratives and historical knowledge. The narrator claims that the word "amoeba" is the Ewe expression *hamueba* which the Mother Goddess uttered when she saw human beings emerge from water, and links this to the beginning of life. There is a resemblance

---

13   A religious association related to the neo-traditionalist mission Afrikania that was established in Ghana in 1982 by the former Catholic priest Kwabena Damuah. Damuah intended to make traditional religion "relevant to our times" by revitalising and up-dating it, and giving it national and pan-African dimensions (De Witte 2008: 135, 231). Other organisations that strengthen local indigenous forms of religion are for example the Asomdwee Fie, Shrine of the Abosom and Nsamanfo International (AFSANI) led by Nana Akua Kyerewaa Opokuwaa, and the SANKORE Foundation directed by Faiza Ibrahim Taimako (see Online Sources for AFSANI and SANKORE websites). Together with other similar organisations, these foundations join national and international groups such as the Ghana Psychic and Traditional Healers Association and the National Association of Certified Natural Health Professionals.

14   Note that "local knowledge" in Datey-Kumodzie (2006), and "modern" mythical narrative means pre/other than Christian/Islamic religions and European/Arabic philosophies and science.

but there is no semantic connection to serve as a basis for asserting an etymological link. Similarly, he claims that the term *hogbe* which the Ewes use to refer to *Amedzɔfe* "the place where humans originated" is related to two present day geographical areas in Eweland: the Ho area and what he calls the Gbe area. The unfortunate thing is that the group which he refers to as the Gbe are actually called the Gbi and there is no linguistic reason that could explain the modification from "e" into "i". Elsewhere he links the name Khartoum to an Ewe expression that seemingly sounds like it. In the same way he claims that the Ewes were in Egypt and that Greek philosophy and Roman thought—as well as Catholicism and Buddhism— were all influenced and in fact were off-shoots of Ewe civilisation, and he buttresses this point with some spurious etymologies.

History

The hypothetical reconstruction of world history and Ewe migrations is his personal narrative. It is problematic if understood as "history" in the sense of the academic discipline, as a reconstruction on the basis of historiographic methods. The interviewee refers to accepted "historical facts" as bricks of his construction and as evidence to give legitimacy to his narration. The problem is that he uses these facts freely and not in the historical or archaeological frames to which they belong. Not only is chronology mixed up at times, but there is also the integration of the Lost Continent of Mu in global history. It is worth recollecting that the Lost Continent of Mu was theorised by Augustus Le Plongeon (1896) and James Churchward (1926, 1931). They claimed the existence of an ancient continent which disappeared in the Atlantic Ocean. Today archaeological, linguistic and genetic evidence has lead scholars to dismiss such a hypothesis and to see it as a fictional narrative.[15] Similarly, the idea that the Ewes together with the Akan, Ashanti and Ga would have migrated from Ethiopia to Egypt in ancient times is in the field of speculation if not fiction. The migration of the Ewes from East Africa and Ethiopia specifically, is also a controversial hypothesis that has been refuted by recent research.[16]

---

15 See Fagan (2006: 23–46).
16 "Some students of Ewe history have tried to push this supposed point of departure [Ketu/Benin] back to Belebele which is in turn identified with the 'Babel' of the Bible. Others have suggested Mesopotamia, Egypt etc., as the point of origin of the Ewes. There is, however, no scientific basis for all these claims" (Amenumey 1997: 14).

Problematic positions of researchers

The problems encounterd raise several issues for research, some of which go beyond the immediate concerns of authorship. One of the issues is that of "insider" and "outsider" researchers, but it transcends that. Merolla is evidently an outsider, but we are also confronted with different kinds of insiders. The interviewee is an insider who is now both a researcher and a researched, Dorvlo is an insider (as an Anlo) but a researcher, while Ameka is an Ewe insider but an Anlo outsider (as a researcher). Moreover, all the participants in the current discourse about the interview belong to the academic world and in this regard they are "outsiders" *vis-à-vis* Ewe local religious knowledge and migration narratives, although (again) they are differently located: Merolla, Ameka and Dorvlo work in the academy, while the interviewee belongs to it as a PhD holder and an independent researcher, but he has not been an active academic for many years now.

Watching the interview over and over again reminds us of the observations the Ghanaian anthropologist Owusu made some decades ago about early African ethnographies, "frequently, it is not clear whether the accounts so brilliantly presented are about native realities at all or whether they are about informants, about scientific models and imaginative speculations or about the anthropologists themselves and their fantasies" (1978: 312).

As a native speaker scholar, Ameka cannot help but think that the narrative is full of the "imaginative speculations" and "fantasies" of the interviewee rather than "native realities". Ameka is also confronted with the fact that should his name be associated with this story, it would give it a certain legitimacy, while the evidentiary bases of most of the interviewee's claims are often blatantly false, and many lay native speakers can show this to be the case.

Merolla is troubled by the clash between the interviewee's attempt to legitimise his narrative (through etymological evidence, historical reconstruction, and the interview itself) and the researchers' knowledge and standards required to distinguish academic discourse from such a hybrid mixing of creation myths, popularising narratives and scientific/ historical knowledge. By selecting the video fragments according to our discourse, "are we simply positivist?" she asks, and unable to give room to difference and alternative cultural constructions?

Both Ameka and Merolla agree that the interview has to be studied and presented as a piece of narrative performance. It is a narrative performance in which the mythopoetic approach deploys itself, but it also appears as a personal mythopoetics built with elements from local—either shared or secret—knowledge. The problem with it is that it has to be understood in the context of a suspended world, as in another world, although the interviewee does not present it as such. If it were presented as a *gli*, a folktale, belonging to a make-believe world, it would have a different status. But it is presented as real/scientific, as knowledge that has to be believed as being truthful and that contends with scientific knowledge for defining and understanding the field of reality. This is the reason why we need to present it in a cautious way when we produce a video documentation intended not only for scholars but also for students and a large public.

Ethical problems

The ethical problem is directly linked to what has been discussed before. We intend to respect our interviewee's discourse, but cannot propose his narrative as such. Not only can we not propose it integrally without enclosing it in comments on the scientific problems mentioned above, but we also cannot avoid selecting the video fragments very carefully, because we offer this as material for students and a large audience who may not yet have the training and the critical stance to interpret this video narrative as a making of tradition.

The selection of the fragment involves another ethical problem as well. As a construction of the researchers' perspective and discourse, it expresses the unbalanced power relationship between the interviewers and the interviewee, given the respective positions in the interview, in academia, and in the present chapter too.

Personal or shared cultural knowledge?

The last point to discuss is whether the interviewee expresses his personal reinterpretation or if it is somehow shared, maybe secret, knowledge among a certain milieu of Ewes. It is evident that his narrative and style is his own. However, interviews conducted in November 2009 in Anloga, traditionally the ritual and political capital of the Anlo-Ewe in Ghana, with some educated Ewes (teachers and office workers) show that the idea that Ewes migrated from Ethiopia to Egypt before reaching West Africa is well-known and it is often presented as historical fact. Although there is little archaeological or linguistic evidence for it, as indicated above, in the diffusion of such an idea we might see the influence of a schoolbook such as *Eve Kɔnuwo*, "Ewe Customs", in which the author S. J. Obianim discusses such an origin as a possibility.

As can be seen in the quotes below, in the introduction to *Eve Kɔnuwo*, first published in 1953 with a second edition in 1956, reissued in 1990, Obianim notes that black Africans originate from Sudan near Egypt and the Abyssinian highlands.[17] Perhaps the Ewes, who are also a part of the black race may have stayed in a part of this land [...] (Obianim 1990: 2).

Obianim then suggests that the Ewes may also have partaken in the great civilisations of the Egyptians:

Perhaps the Ewes learnt some things from them, such as pottery, blacksmithing and different kinds of other crafts. Maybe in the area of customs too, they may have observed how the Pharaoh reigned and how his subjects showed respect to him. [...] Because of the troubles caused by enemy or hostile people [such as slave traders] all the groups/nations who used to be in Sudan near Egypt and the Abyssinian region migrated from there, and there were only few left. Some of the ones who migrated headed east, and others went west.

The Ewes also headed west. After the fall of the Egyptian kingdom, the Ghana Empire rose in its place with its capital at Walata near Timbuktu. The Ewes were also part of this empire and they got some customs from there also. There is no literature confirming this but there are some signs in our language and practices which show that our ancestors knew something about this kingdom [...]. (Ibid.: 2)

After the Ghana Empire, the Mali Empire came in its place and the Songhai Empire also destroyed it: It is clear that the Ewes were also in the Empire. The word for lion in Ewe is *dzata*. It is clear that we gave the name of Mari Dzata to this fierce animal [...] (Obianim 1990: 2–3).[18]

---

17   The quotes are translated by Ameka. It is probably worth noting that the author Obianim comes from Avatime, a mission post of the Bremen mission. Incidentally, the Avatime speak a language called Siya, or Sideme by the Avatimes, which is not mutually intelligible with Ewe. But because of contact with Ewes and also because of the mission schools, almost all Avatime are bilingual at least in Avatime and Ewe. Part of Obianim's knowledge therefore comes from the schooling he received and probably also from the Black renaissance movement and the influential ideas of Cheikh Anta Diop.

18   Mari Dzata is probably for "Mari Djata", one of the names of the hero of the Malian epos Sunjata.

When this kingdom also fell, all the inhabitants dispersed:

> Thus the Ewes also set off northwest until they reached Dahome (now Benin). Here the Ewes divided into two big groups: one part went northeastwards to the Adele region on Dogbo land. The important groups/states that were in this group are the Anlos, the Be, the Agu and the Fon, but the Fon migrated again eastwards into Dahome and established the Fon state. The second big group went southwestwards and divided into two groups: one group stayed in Tado and the other group settled in Notsie. (Ibid.: 1–3)

The influence of schoolbooks is far reaching and goes beyond national boundaries and generation shift. For example, the reconstruction of human history in terms of Ewe worldwide migrations is shared by Togolese Ewes who produced a video summarising the creation and migration narrative of the Ewe, similar to the narrative offered in the interview presented here. Such a video was aired on the Supreme Master Television (28 July 2007) that broadcasts the teachings and actions of their spiritual leader Ching Hai.[19] The video found its way onto the World Wide Web (Figure 1).[20]

Although the aim of the Ewe creation and migration story aired on the Supreme Master Television is unclear, the video appears to assert the centrality of Ewe cosmology and religious/philosophical knowledge in human global history. As in a paper by the interviewee (Datey-Kumodzie 2006), the Ewe/African local knowledge foundation is seen as being central to new technical and spiritual developments in Africa. One wonders whether they do not have the same agenda and whether Dr. Datey-Kumodzie's work was the source of the video.[21]

---

19 The Vietnamese spiritual woman leader Ching Hai developed her meditation method and esoteric knowledge in the 1980s. She appears to have learnt her spiritual path from Thakar Singh, who had the role of Guru at Sawan Asham in Delhi in the late 1970s. Ching Hai founded the Supreme Master Ching Hai International Association (with headquarters in Taiwan), a corporate entity that has a media empire as well as restaurants and a fashion business worldwide. The Association also undertakes charitable activities. The Association and Ching Hai—as painter and fashion designer—have a million dollar business, but the source of the wealth is unclear according to researcher Patricia M. Thornton. Thornton (2003) writes that the Supreme Master Ching Hai International Association relies on the Internet for self-promotion, recruitment and donation, and it can be seen as a transnational "cybersect".

20 See Online Sources for the YouTube clip Abibitumi Kasa website forum.

21 Recent fieldwork shows that the ideas expressed in the YouTube video and by Dr. Datey-Kumodzie find wide resonance in lectures offered at high schools at Anloga town in the Ewe region (Dorvlo and Merolla's personal observation).

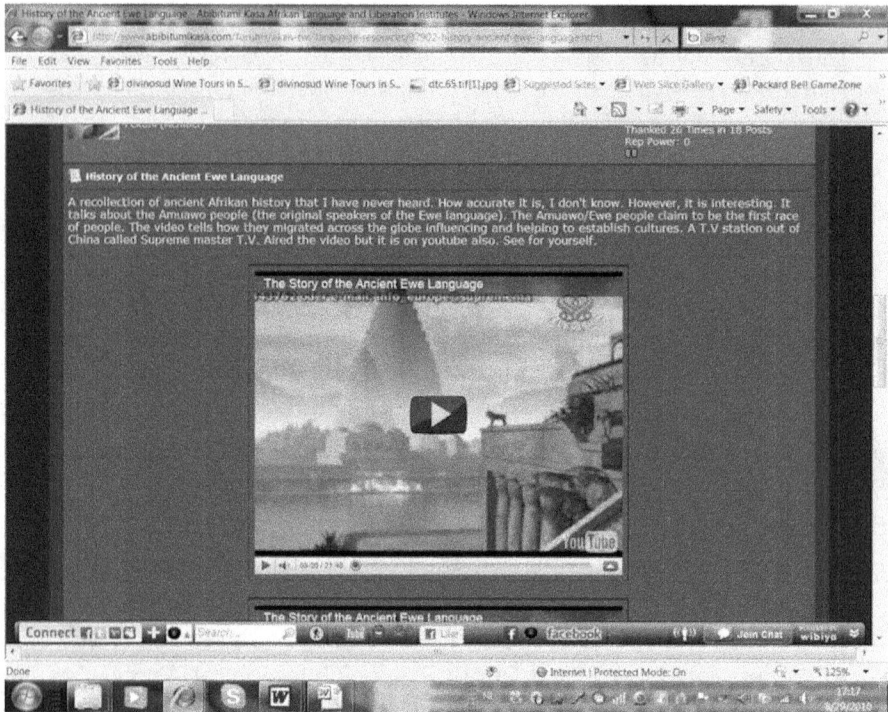

Figure 1.   Screenshot from website of the Abibitumi Kasa Afrikan Language and Liberation Institutes, Forum, Thread "History of the Ancient Ewe Language".[22] Image by Felix Ameka and Daniela Merolla, 2012.

Theoretical reflections and open questions

The study of oral genres has shifted attention from the academic process of recreating the text to the interaction of the participants—that is—from the performers to the researchers, in the performance.[23] This shift in focus has progressively involved the discussion of concepts such as giving voice to informants and authorship in the documentation of oral genres. Such a discussion is indeed urgent when we use video recordings, as in the case presented here, because new technologies are not only tools for recording events but also tools that affect and change what is recorded (Gee and Hayes 2011).

---

22   See Online Sources for the Abibitumi Kasa website.
23   We would like to thank Jan Jansen, Leiden University for this formulation.

On giving voice

Scholars know that the use of video cameras may affect the performance and the context in which they operate. Moreover, the apparent objectivity of video images risks obfuscating perspectives, aims, audiences, and selection processes conveyed by the images. This is quite a confusing and paradoxical situation as we are somehow required to deconstruct our research and video recordings before we have even constructed them.

To summarise our progress so far, we may recollect some effects of the literary analysis of narrative strategies applied to "scientific" writings at the beginning of the 1990s. Anthropologists and historians have used the analysis of perspective and narrative voice very effectively to criticise the way in which classic ethnographies and works of history construct dominant discourses under the guise of objectivity. Anthropologists in particular recognised that informants' voices were subsumed by the researcher's dominant discourse not only in colonial work but also in the recent and most well-intended ethnographies (Appadurai 1991; Augé 1994; Cliffords and Marcus 1986; Crapanzano 1980; Fabian 1983; Geertz 1973 and 1988; Rosaldo 1989 and Rabinaw 1988). Moreover, the very same idea of giving voice to informants appeared to originate in the misconstruction of the disproportionate distance established between subject (researcher) and object (informant) of research. The new approach showed that the seemingly progressive endeavour of giving voice to informants ultimately denied the processes and effects of interactions, negotiations and adaptations taking place in the interview as well as in the process of recording oral genres. On the contrary, recorded interviews and ethnographic writing are rather to be understood as encounter and exchange. A possible resolution may be to pay careful attention to interactions and negotiations and make explicit where the researcher's voice and perspective is constructed and how, when, and where these take the upper hand in the documentation and in the interpretation. As we have seen, however, these indications still leave problems in the recording and video research and documentation.

On authorship

Philosophical and literary studies declared the author "dead" as far back as the 1970s,[24] but questions of authorship and rights persist all the same. New

---

24   We can extrapolate that in Foucault's approach (1969/1994), intellectual property does

electronic media—in particular the Internet and World Wide Web—have opened up very animated discussions on authorship and intellectual property, and even fiercer debates as far as copyright and legal issues are concerned.

A well-known case is exemplified by the discussions on authorship as a collaborative enterprise. New media art is usually created in a very strongly collaborative manner, but tensions arise—sometimes with complicated legal consequences—as "occasionally artists mistakenly claw back to individual authorship when in fact, the final work is highly dependent on their deep collaboration with computer scientists, designers and all manner of other talents" (Diamond 2003).[25] Similar tensions traverse the scientific arena, as cooperation between researchers, technicians and people from business enterprises also generates concerns on intellectual property and authorship. The point is to understand the breadth and depth of the collaboration: who has the intellectual initiative and the intellectual property and, obviously, who can claim the property rights, particularly when products are on the market to be sold and bought.

Another discussion of interest here relates to the rights of indigenous people with regard to knowledge and verbal and visual art forms. The question of intellectual property and the rights of indigenous people developed from the experience of expropriation during and after European expansionism and colonialism, when not only lands and resources but also material and immaterial knowledge and arts were exploited to the advantage of museums, universities, international organisations and enterprises, individual scholars and businessmen. The United Nations Declaration on the Rights of Indigenous Peoples in 2007 states that "Indigenous peoples have the right to revitalize, use, develop and transmit to future generations their histories, languages, oral traditions, philosophies, writing systems and literatures, and to designate and retain their own names for communities, places and persons" (Article 13). Such rights are also to be implemented in political, legal and administrative ways.[26] This UN declaration is interpreted and fought for legally in terms

---

not apply to the "author", as the text is created in an intertextual exchange of ideas and writings belonging to a certain period and society: "no individual can be pointed to as the only source of an idea, as it emerges within far too complex a social and cultural milieu to make any individual imputation sensible" (Longo and Magnolo 2009: 835). Barthes (1968/1984) further disconnects text and author and attributes authorship to the reader who constructs meaning, understanding and unity of the text.

25   See also Manovich (2004).

26   Article 11.2 states: "States shall provide redress through effective mechanisms, which may include restitution, developed in conjunction with indigenous peoples, with respect

of intellectual property, copyright and economic proceedings when, for example, the so-called imitation industry exploits "dreaming designs" of Australian aboriginal people for commercial gain without authorisation and without recognising the copyright and economic damage made to the Aboriginal dreamers/artists.[27] It also stimulates projects of cultural revitalisation, such as the *!Khwa ttu: San Culture & Education Centre* created to counter the impact of so-called ethno-tourism, with game resorts making a profit on staged encounters between tourists and San families who—without equitable contracts and respect—are to "act like 'wild Bushmen'" using loincloths and posing and dancing on demand.[28] As summarised by Staehelin (2002) on Cultural Survival,[29] the *!Khwa ttu* project intends to implement "a concept more ambitious than the mere sale of crafts".[30] We read on their website that *!Khwaa ttu* intends:

> Restore and display San heritage, culture, folklore, visual arts, cosmology and languages; Educate the general public about the world of the San; Provide training to the San in literacy, entrepreneurship, tourism, health issues, community development, craft production/marketing and gender awareness.[31]

Although these are well meant projects that one can only hope will work out as planned, we need to remain aware that the concepts of indigenous rights and copyright are problematic. The concept of "indigenous people" in postcolonial Africa is very complex and confounding and we could rather think in terms of minorities/majorities or marginalised/central (governing) peoples who, after all, are the indigenous people in Ghana. If all groups are indigenous, some groups are more marginalised than others

---

to their cultural, intellectual, religious and spiritual property taken without their free, prior and informed consent or in violation of their laws, traditions and customs". Article 13.2 states: "States shall take effective measures to ensure that this right is protected and also to ensure that indigenous peoples can understand and be understood in political, legal and administrative proceedings, where necessary through the provision of interpretation or by other appropriate means". Article 31.2 states "In conjunction with indigenous peoples, States shall take effective measures to recognize and protect the exercise of these rights". See Online Sources.

27 See Wardrop (2002/2007).

28 "Overseas visitors (the new age fauna), filmmakers, and assorted entrepreneurs were invading remote Bushmen communities with demands that San act like 'wild Bushmen' or pose with consumer products in commercials". From the Cultural Survival website (see Online Sources).

29 See Online Sources for Cultural Survival.

30 See footnote 28.

31 See Online Sources for hyperlinks "Evolve" and "Mission and Background" on the !Khwa ttu website.

and often multi/inter-ethnic elite groups govern.[32] Moreover, the projects mentioned above are framed within the European-developed concept and legal practice of authorship and copyright. Such a frame affects the way verbal/visual genres are re-interpreted and imagined by activists, local people, and international partners alike in terms of art and heritage while undergoing processes of simplification, standardisation, and hybridisation for present aims and constructions.

A challenging question arises when we consider the documentation of oral genres through video and the Internet in light of previous debates: What do "giving voice" and "collaborative authorship" mean in our specific case?

The interview: collaborative authorship vs. researchers as griots

In the case of the interview presented in the Verba Africana series, from a simply collaborative authorship ("collaborative" as in the cases when the interviewee is author together with the interviewers) we have to shift to a more complicated form of authorship, in which interview credits are obviously not a problem, but we as researchers play a decisive, if open, role in the way the discourse is presented.

A more useful framework for looking at this video documentation is that of participant structure introduced by the sociologists Erving Goffman (1981) and its elaborations in, for example, Levinson (1988) and also Hill and Irvine (1993).[33] In this conception there is a principal (who is the source of information or text) and an addressee or recipient. But the principal need not be the one who words the information. It may be done by an animator who "gives the principal his/her voice". This framework has been fruitfully used in the analysis of third party communication or communication involving intermediaries, such as in the analysis of the role of griots. We think our role is that of the animator and in the context of triadic communication in Africa acting like the spokesperson of the principal. In this case, the principal is the interviewee and we, Merolla and Ameka, are the animators or editors who shape and polish, embellish, and retouch offensive language in more palatable language and communicate it through the medium of Verba Africana to the outside world: the addressees. In this

---

32   See Bowen (2000: 12–16).
33   See Yankah (1995) and Ameka (2004) for its application to triadic communication.

way there is distributed authorial responsibility, although we take the lion's share for the effect and any consequences generated by the content we disseminate. We are thus shielding the principal from any attack. Our suggestion of a participant structure approach to the question of authorship and authorial responsibility might go a long way towards clarifying some of the dilemmas in the area of the so-called collaborative authorship. The dilemma is whether the principal — the interviewee — would agree with this perspective on the situation. By virtue of the fact that we have edited the material and are putting the material into the world we have a certain responsibility, moral or otherwise.

At the end

As Augé writes (1994/1999: 48), "the distance between the investigator and the object of the investigation does not represent a mere bias [...] but rather a constraint" that the researchers should negotiate. The provocative idea of "researchers as griots" distances us from the idea of the egalitarian positioning of researchers and storytellers in research and documentation (Fabian 1990), because it presents the interviewee as the Principal and the researcher as the animator and intermediary between the interviewee and the wider community. It suggests that scholars take responsibility towards storytellers and audience(s) and their three-sided interaction in more complex ways, both scientifically and ethically, than was previously advocated or implemented. The interaction of local and globalising forms of knowledge is an increasing phenomenon in Africa, such as in the present example where all the persons involved in the oral performance and its video documentation belong to the academic/educative field, although with different positions and roles. In such a case, the forms, strategies and aims of the "glocal" (local and globalised) knowledge of the storyteller need to be explained to the audience in a form more mediated and critical than the video documentation of oral genres usually does. The "researchers as griots" thus select the video fragments to mediate (or protect) the communication between interviewee and audience, and only offer the whole text of the interview with explicative comments.[34]

---

34 We would like to thanks the participants of the conference *Archiving Orality and Connecting with Communities: World Oral Literature Project 2010 Workshop*, CRASSH, Cambridge, UK for the suggestions to use a new format including several video fragments in the same frame, so that different perspectives (also those of the researchers) can be heard. The need remains for the researchers to select and to mediate the communication between

When we re-read the interview and our selection in light of indigenous rights and new media collaborative authorship, we see that our case opens up an important point: indigenous rights are not individual rights so that no one individual is expected to be a self-appointed advocate for the group. This means that we need to reflect on internal discordances and diversities and to make use of the criticism raised about collectivistic concepts such as tradition and heritage, and to encourage the "grand" institutions to become less populist in their approaches to collaborative work and indigenous rights.

Finally, we think that—notwithstanding (or maybe as a direct result of) the problems encountered—the video documentation of the interview discussed here offers a most interesting contemporary form of local knowledge that is adapted and invented in a creative and esoteric way to respond to social and cultural processes, including the increasing importance and assertiveness of Christianity and Islam in West Africa, nationalism, globalisation and glocalising developments. The presence of a YouTube video with similar content increases the interest related to the oral-written-electronic interactions in ongoing identity negotiations and creations.

References

Aduamah, E. Y., *Ewe Tradition, No. 1* (Legon: Institute of African Studies, University of Ghana, 1965).

Ameka, F. K., 'Grammar and Cultural Practices: The Grammaticalisation of Triadic Communication in West African Languages', *Journal of West African Languages*, 30 (2) (2004), 5–28.

Amenumey, D. E. K., 'A Brief History', in *A Handbook of Eweland. The Ewes of Southeastern Ghana*, vol. I, ed. by F. Agbodeka (Accra: Woeli Publishing Services 1997), 14–27.

Anyidoho, K., 'The Back Without Which There Is No Front', *Africa Today*, 50 (2) (2005), 3–18.

Appadurai, A, 'Global Ethnoscapes: Notes and Queries for a Transnational Anthropology', in *Recapturing Anthropology*, ed. by R. Fox (Santa Fe: School of American Research Press, 1991).

Augé, M., *Pour une anthropologie des mondes contemporains* (Paris: Aubier, 1994). trans. *An Anthropology for Contemporaneous Worlds* (California: Stanford University Press, 1999).

---

the "Principal" and the third party in the production of a video documentation freely accessible on the Internet as the Verba African series is.

Barber, Karin, ed., *Readings in African Popular Culture* (London: The International African Institute, SOAS; and Oxford: Curry, 1997).

Barthes, R., 'La mort de l'Auteur', in *Le bruissement de la langue*, ed. by R. Barthes (Paris: Seuil, 1968/1984), 61–67.

Baumgardt, Ursula and Abdellah Bounfour, eds., *Panorama des littératures africaines* (Paris: L'Harmattan, 2000).

Bowen, J. R., 'Should We have a Universal Concept of Indigenous Peoples' Rights?: Ethnicity and Essentialism in the Twenty-first Century', *Anthropology Today*, 16 (4) (2000), 12–16.

Churchward, James, *Children of Mu* (New York: Ives Washburn, 1931).

—, *The Lost Continent of Mu: the Motherland of Man* (New York: Ives Washburn, 1926).

Cliffords, J. and G. E. Marcus, *Writing Culture* (Los Angeles/ London: University of California Press, 1986).

Coulet Western, Dominique, *A Bibliography of the Arts of Africa* (Waltham, MA: African Studies Association of Brandeis University, 1975).

Crapanzano, V., *Tuhami: Portrait of a Moroccan* (Chicago: University of Chicago Press, 1980).

Datey-Kumodzie, S., *Musik und die Yeweh- oder Hu-Religion. Der Sogbo-Musikkult* (unpublished doctoral dissertation, Universität zu Köln, 1989).

—, 'Finding a Knowledge Foundation for Africa', *Inter-generational Forum on Endogenous Governance in West Africa, Working Documents, Vol. 2* (Issy-Les Moulineaux: OECD, 2006), 111–127. <http://www.oecd.org/dataoecd/59/26/38516561.pdf> [Accessed 24 October 2012].

—, Interview, fragments published in Merolla, D., F. Ameka, and K. Dorvlo 'Verba Africana No.5: Hogbetsotso: The Celebration and Songs of the Ewe Migration Stories' in *Verba Africana Series*, ed. by Daniela Merolla (Leiden: Leiden University and University of Ghana, 2011). <www.hum2.leidenuniv.nl/verba-africana/> [Accessed 24 October 2012].

De Witte, M., *Spirit Media-charismatics, traditionalists, and mediation practices in Ghana* (unpublished doctoral dissertation, University of Amsterdam, 2008).

Diamond, S., *Curating the Flow—the Challenges of Collaborative Exchange and the New Media* (Emily Carr University of Art and Design, 2003). <www.ecuad.ca/~rburnett/curating.pdf> [Accessed 26 November 2009; URL no longer accessible].

Fabian, J., *Power and Performance, Ethnographic Explorations through Proverbial Wisdom and Theater in Shaba Zaire* (Madison: University of Wisconsin, 1990).

—, *Time and the Other: How Anthropology Makes Its Subject* (New York: Columbia University Press, 1983).

Fagan, G. G., 'Diagnosing Pseudoarchaelogy', in *Archaeological Fantasies*, ed. by G. G. Fagan (London and New York: Routledge, 2006), 23–46.

Fianu, D. D., *The Hoawo and the Gligbaza Festival of the Asogli State of Eweland: A Historical Sketch* (Self-published, 1986).

Finnegan, Ruth, *Oral Traditions and the Verbal Arts* (London/New York: Routledge, 1992).

Foucault, M., 'Qu'est-ce qu'un auteur?', in *Dits et ecrits 1954–1988, vol. I, 1954–1969*, ed. by D. Defert and F. Ewald (Paris: Gallimard, 1969/1994), 789–821.

Furniss, Graham, *Poetry, prose and popular culture in Hausa* (Edinburgh/London: Edinburgh University Press for the International African Institute, 1996).

Gayibor, N. L. and A. Aguigah, 'Early Settlements and Archaeology of the Adja-Tado Culture Zone', in *The Ewe of Togo and Benin*, ed. by B. N. Lawrence (Accra: Woeli Publishing Services, 2005), 1–13.

—, 'Agpkoli et la dispersion des Ewe de Notsé', in *Peuples du Golfe du Bénin*, ed. by F. De Medeiros (Paris: Karthala et Centre de Recherches Africaines, 1984), 21–34.

—, 'Le remodelage des traditions historiques: la légende d'Agokoli, roi de Notse', in *Source orales de l'histoire de l'Afrique*, ed. by C.-H. Perrot, G. Gonnin, and F. Nahimana (Paris: CNRS, 1989), 209–214.

Gee, J. P. and E. R. Hayes, *Language and Learning in the Digital Age* (London: Routledge, 2011).

Geertz, C., *The Interpretation of Cultures* (New York: Basic, 1973).

—, *Works and Lives. The Anthropologist as Author* (California: Standford University Press, 1988).

Goffman, E., *Forms of Talk* (Philadelphia: University of Pennsylvania Press, 1981).

Görög-Karady, V., 'Tales and Ideology: The Revolt of Sons in Bambara-Malinké Tales', in *Power, Marginality and African Oral Literature*, ed. by G. Furniss and L. Gunner (Cambridge: Cambridge University Press, 1995), 83–91.

—, *Littérature orale d'Afrique noire: bibliographie analytique* (Paris: Maisonneuve et Larose, 1981).

Greene, S. E., 'Notsie Narratives: History, Memory, and Meaning in West Africa', in *The South Atlantic Quaterly*, 101 (4) (2002a), 1015–1041.

—, *Sacred Sites and the Colonial Encounter: A History of Meaning and Memory in Ghana* (Bloomington: Indiana University Press, 2002b).

Hartter, G., J. Spieth and G. Daeuble, *Ewegbalehlela fe Sukuwe IV* [Ewe Syllabi] (Bremen: Norddeutsche Missionsgesellschaft, 1906).

Hill, J. H. and J. T. Irvine, eds., *Responsibility and Evidence in Oral Discourse* (Cambridge: Cambridge University Press, 1993).

Kwakume, H., *Précis d'histoire du peuple evhe* (Lomé: Ecole Professionnelle, 1948).

Lawrence, B. N., ed., *The Ewe of Togo and Benin* (Accra: Woeli Publishing Services, 2005).

Le Plongeon, Augustus, *Queen Moo and the Egyptian Sphinx* (New York: Kessinger Publishing, 1896).

Levinson, S. C., 'Putting Linguistics on a Proper Footing: Explorations in Goffman's Participation Framework'. In *Goffman, Exploring the Interaction Order*, ed. by P. Drew and A. Wootton (Oxford: Polity Press, 1988), 161–227.

Longo, M. and S. Magnolo, 'The Author and Authorship in the Internet Society. New Perspectives for Scientific Communication', *Current Sociology*, 57 (2009), 829–850.

Mamattah, C. M. K., *The Ewes of West Africa* (Ghana: Advent Press, 1979).

Merolla, D., 'Digital Imagination and the 'Landscapes of Group Identities': Berber Diaspora and the Flourishing of Theatre, Videos, and Amazigh-Net', *The Journal of North African Studies* (Winter 2002), 122–131.

—, 'Migrant Websites, WebArt, and Digital Imagination', in *Migrant Cartographies, New Cultural and Literary Spaces in Post-colonial Europe*, ed. by S. Ponzanesi and D. Merolla (USA: Lexington Books, 2005), 217–228.

Nukunya, G. K., 'Festivals', in *A Handbook of Eweland, The Ewes of Southeastern Ghana*, ed. by F. Agbodeka (Accra: Woeli Publishing Services, 1997), 105–122.

Obianim, S. J., *Eve Kɔnuwo* (Accra: Sedco Publishing, 1990).

Okpewho, Isidoro, *African Oral Literature* (Bloomington and Indianapolis: Indiana University Press, 1992).

Owuso, M., 'Ethnography of Africa, The Usefulness of the Useless', *American Anthropologist*, 80 (1978), 310– 334.

Paulme, D., *La mere dévorante* (Paris: Gallimard, 1976).

Pazzi, R., *Notes d'histoire des peuples aja, éwé, gen et fon* (Lomé: ORSTOM, 1973).

Rabinaw, P., 'Beyond Ethnography: Anthropology as Nominalism', *Cultural Anthropology*, 3 (3) (1988), 335–364.

Ricard, Alain and Flora Veit-Wild, eds., *Interfaces Between the Oral and the Written/ Interfaces entrel'écrit et l'oral, Matatu Series* (Amsterdam: Rodopi, 2005).

Rosaldo, R., *Culture and Truth: The Remaking of Social Analysis* (Boston: Beacon Press, 1989).

Schipper, M., *Imagining Insiders: Africa and the Question of Belonging* (London and New York: Cassell, 1999).

—, *Afrikaanse Letterkunde* (Gravenhage: AMBO, 1990).

Staehelin, Irene, '!Khwa ttu: San Culture & Education Centre, Cultural and Survival', *Culture and Survival Quaterly* "The Kalahari San", 26.1 (2002), online April 28, 2010 <http://www.culturalsurvival.org/ourpublications/csq/article/khwa-ttu-san-culture-education-centre> [Accessed 5 September 2012]

Thornton, P. M., 'The New Cybersects: Resistance and Repression in the Reform Era', in *Chinese Society: Change, Conflict and Resistance* (2nd edition), ed. by Elizabeth Perry and Mark Selden (London and New York: Routledge, 2003), 247–270.

Yankah, K., *Speaking for the Chief: Okyeame and the Politics of Akan Royal Oratory*, (Bloomington: Indiana University Press, 1995).

Online Sources

Abibitumi Kasa website forum
<http://www.abibitumikasa.com/forums/afrikan-spiritual-systems/>

Abibitumi Kasa website forum, *History of the Ancient Ewe Language*
<www.abibitumikasa.com/forums/akan-twi-language-resources/37902-history-ancient-ewe-language.html>

Asomdwee Fie, Shrine of the Abosom and Nsamanfo International (AFSANI) led by Nana Akua Kyerewaa Opokuwaa
<http://www.afsani.org/nanakyerewaa/aboutauthor.htm>

Cultural Survival
  <www.culturalsurvival.org>

Cultural Survival, *!Khwa ttu: San Culture & Education Centre*
  <www.culturalsurvival.org/ourpublications/csq/article/khwa-ttu-san-culture-education-centre>

!Khwa ttu

Leiden University, *African literatures*
  <http://www.hum.leiden.edu/research/africanliteratures>

Leiden University, *Verba Africana series*
  <www.hum2.leidenuniv.nl/verba-africana/>

Manovich, L. 2004. *Who is the Author?: Sampling/Remixing/Open Source*
  <www.manovich.net/DOCS/models_of_authorship.doc>

SANKORE Foundation
  <http://www.sankorefoundation.org/sankore-about.html>

United Nations (2007), *Declaration on the Rights of Indigenous Peoples*
  <http://www.ohchr.org/EN/Issues/IPeoples/Pages/Declaration.aspx>

Wardrop, M. June (2002; updated 2007). Copyright and Intellectual Property Protection for Indigenous Heritage, Aboriginal Art Online
  <www.aboriginalartonline.com/resources/debate.php>

YouTube, *The Story of the Ancient Ewe Language*
  <http://www.youtube.com/watch?v=dUDrLCB0wQk>

5. American Indian Oral Literature, Cultural Identity and Language Revitalisation: Some Considerations for Researchers

Margaret Field

The Kumeyaay community of Baja California

Kumeyaay is the indigenous language of the San Diego area as well as the northernmost part of Baja California, Mexico, extending southward from the US-Mexico border for about fifty miles. Today, Kumeyaay (specifically, the Tiipay dialect of Kumeyaay) is still actively spoken by about fifty speakers who reside in Mexico, but is very close to obsolescence north of the border. The Tiipay community extends from about fifty miles east of San Diego to the coast, encompassing thirteen distinct communities, each with its own slightly different variety of Tiipay. Just north of these Tiipay communities are the related 'Iipay Kumeyaay communities, which share many similar cultural values, but whose dialects are very different (Field, 2012).

In all of the Kumeyaay community as well as most of southern California, singers are important repositories of traditional oral literature, as stories are typically not only told but also embodied in song cycles (Apodaca 1999). In the San Diego area, the most well known of these song cycles are "bird songs", which tell the story of early migrations of Yuman people from the Colorado river area throughout southern Alta California, Baja California, and adjacent Arizona. Other song cycles include Lightning songs and Wildcat songs, and this paper will draw on an example of a story

DOI: 10.111647/OBP.0032.06.

told by a master singer of the Wildcat tradition, Jon Meza Cuero. The story is about Rabbit and Frog.[1]

The story "Rabbit and Frog" is probably most closely related to the genre of trickster tales, which are found across all of Native North America, especially in the western part of the US; the most commonly known subgenre being "coyote stories" (Bright 1993). The protagonist in the genre of trickster tales need not always be a coyote, but is always a trickster who displays various kinds of culturally dispreferred behaviors, such as insincerity, gluttony, and above all egotistical narcissism. The Tiipay story of Rabbit and Frog does not feature a coyote, but instead a frog that displays trickster-like characteristics. The other main character is Rabbit, who is duped by the trickster and comes to regret it in the end.

When sung in song cycles, traditional stories like this one bring together two important aspects of communicative competence: cultural knowledge in the form of social values and behavioral norms and expectations, as well as traditional language. Mr Meza Cuero is one of the few Kumeyaay culture bearers today who is able to tell his stories (as opposed to singing them) in the indigenous language as well. Traditional stories are a key part of the process of cultural continuity. As Toelken and Scott have noted in their study of this genre, coyote stories teach children cultural expectations about appropriate behavior through the use of humour "without resort to didacticism" (1981: 106). Storytelling, in this way, is an important part of child socialisation. The cultural knowledge learned through communicative practices such as storytelling includes cultural expectations about social roles and relationships, including, very importantly for indigenous American communities, how to treat family as opposed to strangers. Each of these communicative contexts involves slightly different social roles that may also be associated with distinct communicative strategies.[2] The story of Rabbit and Frog deals with these roles in particular. Forms of knowledge such as these are invariably tacit or taken for granted, and thus less accessible to discursive consciousness (Giddens 1979). Embedded in traditional stories, they provide good examples of what Bourdieu (1977) has called the *habitus*, or "routine modes of perception, action, and evaluation which guide actors in social practice" (Hanks 1996: 238). In this

---

1 See Meza Cuero et al. (2013) for a detailed version and translation of this particular story.
2 See Field (1998) for a discussion of how the pragmatics of directive giving varies across these contexts for Navajo speakers, as well as Nevins (2010) for a discussion of these dynamics in the Apache community.

way, traditional stories and other forms of oral tradition may be viewed as interactional strategies through which cultural identity is discursively produced. Additionally, just as stories act as discourse-level vehicles for the transmission of identity, so does the linguistic variety in which the story is told. Thus, oral literature indexes group identity in multiple ways (Kroskrity 2000) as membership in a larger speech community is indexed through traditional storytelling, yet local dialect indexes membership in a sub-community within that larger speech community.

For many indigenous communities, the dialect in which a story is told is just as valuable to the community as the content of the story, and both require the careful attention of the researcher. This is especially true in indigenous communities where local dialects are important emblems of cultural and group identity. For example, in the Tiipay-speaking Kumeyaay community of Mexico, there are distinct local dialects across six communities, all located within a fifty-mile radius of each other (Field 2012). Intense lexical variation is found in many indigenous Californian and Mexican speech communities (Friedrich 1971; Golla 2000; Field 2012), as well as many other indigenous communities around the world (Sutton 1978), and is closely connected to group identity.

Language ideologies in indigenous communities may also reflect beliefs concerning the relationship between local varieties and community identity, but are not necessarily homogeneous across related speech communities. For example, members of US Kumeyaay communities frequently express the belief that their dialects are each different enough to be considered distinct languages. This attitude exemplifies a typical "localist" language ideology,[3] which is linked to a discourse of "local control" (Hill 2002: 123) often seen in south-western US indigenous speech communities. Kumeyaay tribes on the US side of the border are often hesitant to share language materials, even with each other, let alone academics or non-Kumeyaay people. In contrast, on the Mexican side of the border, community language ideologies are typically more variationist (Kroskrity 2002; Kroskrity and Field 2009), such that everyone acknowledges dialect variation, yet insists that all dialects are mutually intelligible and therefore one language, shared by all. This difference in language ideologies between US and Mexican communities is no doubt largely due to differences in histories of contact with two different

---

3   See Field (2012) for a lengthier discussion of language ideologies in Kumeyaay communities.

dominant cultures, as well as other considerations too lengthy to include here (but see Field 2012). More to the point of this paper, this difference in language ideologies will no doubt have profound repercussions for the development of future materials for language revitalisation purposes, as well as very different considerations for researchers working on these related dialects on each side of the international border.

Although geographically connected communities may share very similar, if not identical, versions of traditional stories, storytellers from specific communities inject their own community's idiom into them, marking them as symbols of local community identity and making them not only very different from each other but clearly indexical of the local community the storyteller is from. These facts lead to a couple of important language-related considerations for researchers of oral literature: firstly, the effects this research may have on language revitalisation efforts; and secondly, the imperative to work collaboratively with the community, and prioritise their wishes concerning access to and future uses of any collected texts. These points are expanded upon below.

Firstly, when archiving and publishing language materials from communities without a tradition of literacy, it is important to be aware that making any materials public may affect language revitalisation efforts in that community. If there is no standard dialect, or orthography, published research may potentially affect what might be a delicate political balance between factions of the speech community, or may have an impact on language maintenance. For example, if materials from only one dialect are published to a greater extent than another, this may result in *de facto* promotion of that one dialect to the status of "standard", and may privilege that variety over others for use in future language revitalisation efforts (Muhlhauser 1996; Hale 2001; Eisenlohr 2004; Hill 2002).

In Native North America, there is today not a single speech community that is not endangered at some level. According to a study by Michael Krauss done a little over a decade ago, out of 211 indigenous languages still spoken in North America, 85% of them are now moribund (or lack child speakers). Ironically, this situation continues to worsen even as indigenous communities improve their economic conditions, because dominant languages and cultures increasingly penetrate even the most remote communities, along with roads, electricity, and greater access to various forms of media in dominant languages.

Secondly, even though the goals of research on oral literatures and endangered languages may be to preserve them for posterity, indigenous communities may not all be in accord with this common academic goal, or with the assumption that all knowledge should be shared (Hill 2002). Intellectual property concerns are always an important consideration for American Indian communities. Even though a recorded story may already be published, the language or dialect in which it is told may not be, and the language itself may be considered intellectual property by the speech community. In the US and Canada it is standard operating procedure when working with indigenous languages to request consent from tribal governments (in addition to individual speakers and storytellers) before beginning fieldwork. As Battiste and Henderson (2000) recommend:

> Ethical research systems and practices should enable indigenous nations, people, and communities to exercise control over information related to their knowledge and heritage and to themselves. […] To act otherwise is to repeat that familiar pattern of decisions being made for Indigenous people by those who presume to know what is best for them. (Cited in Rice 2006: 133)

Ideally, initial contact with the indigenous community should include:

1) Discussion of how any resulting materials may be used to promote or enhance linguistic and cultural maintenance and/or revitalisation effort
2) Plans for publication and archiving, including the content of consent forms specifying exactly what, if any, limitations the community might prefer in terms of future access to recorded materials

Great care should be taken in recording and archiving oral literature for posterity. The website E-MELD (Electronic Metastructure for Endangered Languages Documentation) is one of the best places to find information on how to do this. The main goal of this site is to educate researchers on how to archive their audio and video data in non-proprietary formats, so that it will be universally accessible and will remain that way indefinitely. This site also offers useful information on recommended models of recording equipment and methodologies for archiving recordings and associated metadata. If the indigenous language requires special characters not found on an English keyboard, it is especially important to employ a non-proprietary font in Unicode, so that a decade from now transcribed texts will still be legible.

Rabbit and Frog: a Kumeyaay trickster tale

The Tiipay trickster tale of Rabbit and Frog begins with a formulaic opening that immediately indexes the fact that this story is an ancient example of a cultural resource.[4] This is seen in the archaic language, which cannot be entirely glossed (personal communication Amy Miller).[5] The storyteller Jon Meza Cuero translated (in Spanish) all five of the opening lines as "it's old":

Ke'nápa nyuuchs.	It's an old story.
Nyuuch yúsa.	It's old.
Nyuu,	It's old,
nyuu yus 'i mat.	it's old, I say.
Ke'nápa nyuuch nyáasa:	It's an old story I am telling you:

This formulaic opening is a good example of what Richard Baumann has described as "an act of authentication akin to the [...] antique dealer's authentication of an object by tracing its provenience" (1992: 137). In doing so, the storyteller is explaining that this story has been passed down to him from the ancestors.

The genre is made clear in the next few lines, which indicate that it refers to a mythic time period found across most of Native America, and especially in California creation stories, in which animals figure largely as creators:

Matt 'ekur,	Long ago,
tipay pi tenyewaay,	people were here,
matt pi tenyewaay.	they were in this place.
Tipay máwa,	They were not people,
chiillyich.	they were animals.

---

4   See Baumann (1992); Jahner (1999); and Sekaquaptewa & Washburn (2004) for the importance of oral literature as cultural resources which retain and reinforce cultural values and group identity.

5   I am indebted to noted Yuman linguist Amy Miller for her help in transcribing and translating this story.

Chiillyích pas	they were animals, but
tipay llywíicha.	they were like people.
Tipay aa chuwaay,	They spoke the People's language,
peyii neyiw,	they came,
peyii naa,	and they went,
matt cham naach,	they went all over the world,
Tipay aa shin chuuwaay.	and they spoke the one People's language.

Cultural values are also evidenced in the last line of this orientation, which indexes the variationist language ideology most commonly espoused by the Mexican Kumeyaay community.

The following is a somewhat abbreviated version of the story (see Meza Cuero et al. 2013 for the complete version in both English and Kumeyaay):

There was a Rabbit. He had a house.

Rabbit was in his house, and was warm.

Frog passed by the house.

Frog peeked inside.

Rabbit was sitting inside. He was eating.

Frog passed by and went away.

A few days later, Frog came passing by.

'Hi! How are you?' he said as he arrived.

'I'm fine, and you?' (said Rabbit).

'I'm fine. Gee, it's very cold outside!' (said Frog).

'It's cold? It's nice and warm in here.' (said Rabbit).

'I'm really cold.' (said Frog), rubbing his hands together. 'Gee, it's really cold.'

'Oh?' (said Rabbit). 'Walk around and you'll be alright.'

'You are from outside and you must stay outside. God made you so that you would live outside. I do not, I am a rabbit, and I must stay in my house.'

'Alright, see you soon.' said Frog. 'I'm going now.'

And he went hopping away—hop! hop! hop!

In two or three days, he came back.

'Hello Brother!' he said. 'How are you?'

'I'm fine. How are you?' (asked Rabbit).

'Oh, I'm really cold.' (said Frog).

This exchange happens three times, but the third time, Rabbit changes his mind, lets him in, and goes out to find some food for both of them to eat:

Rabbit went out looking for food.

He came back much later.

'What's up?' (Rabbit) said.

'Nothing, I'm fine here.' (said Frog).

(Rabbit) gave him food, and (Frog) just sat there eating.

'Oh, the food is really good!' (said Frog).

One day went by. Two days went by.

(Rabbit) went out again looking for food.

When it was late he came back.

Frog was just sitting in there, big and puffed up.

'Hello Brother! How are you? Are you sick or something?'
(asked Rabbit).

'No, I'm fine' (Frog said).

'Why are you so big?' (asked Rabbit).

'Why am I big? Everyday you bring me food!

I'm just going to sit here getting fat!' (said Frog).

Three days later, frog was at his biggest.

'Your belly is really very big!' (said Rabbit).

'Oh? So what if it is very big?' (said Frog).

'If I am to fit in the house, you have to leave!' (said Rabbit).

'No, no, it's my house!' (said Frog).

'It's really, really, really good, my belly is very big.' (said Frog).

'Okay then, you stay here, and I'll go away.' (said Rabbit).

He did it very reluctantly.

Frog stayed in the house.

He stayed, and Rabbit went away, looking for another house.

That'll be the end of it, this thing that I've been telling.

As is usually the case in trickster tales, there is no overt evaluation by the storyteller (Beck and Walters 1977; Toelken and Scott 1981); rather, the listeners must infer the moral for themselves. But it is easy to discern the moral of this story: after inviting Frog into his home, industrious Rabbit loses it to the ungrateful and selfish Frog. What did Rabbit do to deserve this fate? He acted against his initial better judgment (concerning frogs belonging outside) and embraced Frog, a relative stranger, as a kinsman and brother. Following traditional Kumeyaay protocol, Rabbit feeds Frog, but Frog just sits there getting fatter and fatter until there is no room for Rabbit in his own home. One can infer from this tale that in the traditional Kumeyaay view it is important to be selective in deciding whom to offer hospitality, as well as to be suspicious of strangers who are quick to claim a kinship relation.

Like any good trickster, Frog also displays several negative behavioral characteristics, including laziness, insincerity and greed. Children learn cultural values from trickster tales by learning how *not* to behave; in this case, from the actions of both the trickster and Rabbit. Stories like this are classic examples of traditional indigenous pedagogy.

The story of Rabbit and Frog was collected as part of a larger project documenting the Kumeyaay dialects spoken in Baja California.[6] It will eventually be archived at the Archive of Indigenous Languages of Latin America at the University of Texas, Austin (AILLA),[7] so that it will be available via the Internet in both Spanish and English to members of the Kumeyaay community on both sides of the border as well as researchers. The decision to make all language files available via the Internet was made by members of the Baja Kumeyaay community, who came together with project staff repeatedly in community language workshops held every three months over the duration of the project. Mexican Kumeyaay community members especially expressed the desire for community teachers to be able to access stories and other recordings[8] for language revitalisation

---

6 This work is based upon material supported by the National Science Foundation under Grant No. # BCS-0753853. Any opinions, findings, and conclusions or recommendations expressed in this material are those of the author and do not necessarily reflect the views of the National Science Foundation.

7 I chose the AILLA archive because of the compatibility of their mission statement with the goals of this project: 1) preservation of indigenous language materials from Latin America, 2) accessibility of these materials (in terms of making sure that non-proprietary formats are used in recording, consent forms are obtained, and intellectual property rights are respected), and 3) community support for the indigenous speech communities of Latin America, in terms of making sure these materials are also available for them to use for language revitalisation purposes.

8 We did not record any ritual language or content considered too sensitive to share with the outside world. In addition to traditional narratives and narratives about how to perform traditional activities such as basket making and pottery, we also recorded conversation and wordlists which will be used to create a multidialectal Kumeyaay dictionary.

purposes. Because this story and others were recorded in both Kumeyaay and Spanish, they will be important for this purpose, but they will also be equally vital as traditional Kumeyaay educational materials that impart more than just linguistic information. In this way, they will be important to future Kumeyaay communities in maintaining not only their language, but their cultural identity as well.

References

Apodaca, Paul, 'Tradition, Myth, and Performance of Cahuilla Bird Songs' (unpublished doctoral dissertation, University of California, 1999).

Battiste, Marie and Sa'ke'j Henderson, *Protecting Indigenous Knowledge and Heritage: A Global Challenge* (Saskatoon, SK: Purich, 2000).

Bauman, Richard, 'Contextualization, Tradition, and the Dialogue of Genres: Icelandic Legends of the Kraftaskald', in *Rethinking Context: Language as an Interactive Phenomenon*, ed. by Alessandro Duranti and Charles Goodwin (Cambridge: Cambridge University Press, 1992), pp. 125–145.

Beck, Peggy and Anna Walters, *The Sacred: Ways of Knowledge, Sources of Life* (Tsaile: Navajo Community College, 1977).

Bourdieu, Pierre, *Outline of a Theory of Practice*, trans. by R. Nice (Cambridge: Cambridge University Press, 1977).

Bright, William, *A Coyote Reader* (Berkeley: University California Press, 1993).

Eisenlohr, Patrick, 'Language Revitalization and New Technologies: Cultures of Electronic Mediation and the Refiguring of Communities', *American Review of Anthropology*, 33 (2004), 21–45.

Field, Margaret, 'Politeness and Indirection in Navajo Directives', *Southwest Journal of Linguistics*, 17 (2) (1998), 23–33.

—, 'Kumiai Stories: Bridges Between the Oral Tradition and Contemporary Classroom Practice', in *Telling Stories in the Face of Danger: Narratives and Language, Renewal in Native American Communities*, ed. by Paul Kroskrity (Norman: University of Oklahoma Press, 2011), pp. 115-128.

—, 'Kumeyaay Language Variation, Group Identity, and the Land', *International Journal of American Linguistics*, 78 (4) (2012), 557–573

Friedrich, Paul, 'Dialectal Variation in Tarascan Phonology', *International Journal of American Linguistics*, 37 (3) (1971), 164–187.

Giddens, Anthony, *Central Problems in Social Theory* (London: Macmillan, 1979).

Golla, Victor, 'Language Histories and Communicative Strategies in Aboriginal California and Oregon', in *Languages of the North Pacific Rim*, Vol 5, ed. by Osahito Miyaoka (Japan: Osaka Gakuin University, 2000), pp. 43-64.

Hale, Kenneth, 'Strict Locality in Local Language Media: An Australian Example', in *The Green Book of Language Revitalization in Practice*, ed. by Leanne Hinton and Ken Hale (San Diego: Academic Press, 2001), pp. 276-282.

Hanks, William, *Language And Communicative Practices* (Boulder, CO: Westview Press, 1996).

Hill, Jane, '"Expert Rhetorics" in Advocacy for Endangered Languages: Who Is Listening, and What Do They Hear?', *Journal of Linguistic Anthropology*, 12 (2) (2002), 119–133.

Jahner, Elaine, 'Traditional Narrative: Contemporary Uses, Historical Perspectives', *Studies in American Indian Literatures*, 11 (2) (Summer 1999), 1–28.

Krauss, Michael, 'The Condition of Native North American Languages: The Need for Realistic Assessment and Action', *International Journal of the Sociology of Language*, 132 (1998), 9–21.

Kroskrity, Paul, 'Regimenting Languages: Language Ideological Perspectives', in *Regimes of Language: Ideologies, Politics, and Identities*, ed. by Paul V. Kroskrity (Santa Fe: School of American Research Press, 2000), 1–34.

—, 'Language Renewal and the Technologies of Literacy and Post-Literacy', in *Making Dictionaries: Preserving Indigenous Languages of the Americas*, ed. by William Frawley, Ken Hill and Pamela Munro (Berkeley, CA: University of California Press, 2002), 171–192.

—, and Margaret Field, *Native American Language Ideologies: Language Beliefs, Practices, and Struggles in Indian Country* (Tucson: University Arizona Press, 2009).

Meza Cuero, Jon, Amy Miller and Margaret Field, *Inside Dazzling Mountains*, ed. by David Kozak (Lincoln and London: University of Nevada Press, 2013).

Muhlhauser, Peter, *Linguistic Ecology: Language Change and Linguistic Imperialism in the Pacific Region* (London: Routledge, 1996).

Nevins, Marybeth Eleanor, *"Speak for Me": Knowledge, Otherness and Speaking Across Contrasting Idioms of Intersubjectivity on the Fort Apache Reservation* (unpublished paper presented at the American Anthropological Association, 2010).

Rice, Keren, 'Ethical Issues in Linguistic Fieldwork: An Overview', *Journal of Academic Ethics*, 4 (2006), 123–155.

Sekaquaptewa, Emory and Dorothy Washburn, 'They Go Along Singing: Reconstructing the Hopi Past from Ritual Metaphors in Song and Image', *American Antiquity*, 69 (3) (2004), 457–486.

Sutton, Peter, *Wik: Aboriginal Society, Territory and Language at Cape Keerweer, Cape York Peninsula, Australia* (unpublished doctoral dissertation, University of Queensland, 1978).

Toelken, Barre and Tacheeni Scott, 'Poetic Retranslation and the Pretty Languages of Yellowman', in *Traditional Literatures of the American Indian: Texts and Interpretations*, ed. by Karl Kroeber (Reno: University Nevada Press, 1981), pp. 65–116.

Online Sources

E-MELD (Electronic Metastructure for Endangered Languages Documentation) <http://emeld.org/school/>

6. Ecuador's Indigenous Cultures: Astride Orality and Literacy

Jorge Gómez Rendón

Indigenous languages in Ecuador: survival and change

Ecuador is the smallest of the Andean countries but is linguistically diverse. Indigenous languages have not successfully entered literacy through educational programmes and are now critically endangered. Eleven indigenous languages from six different language families, including two unclassified ones, are spoken in Ecuador (Gómez Rendón 2009: 7).[1] Kichwa is the most popular indigenous language: it is spoken in the Andean highlands and the Amazon lowlands, and nowadays also in several coastal cities and some towns of the Galapagos Islands as a result of labour migration. While the indigenous population in the highlands is the largest in the country, the indigenous population in the Amazon lowlands is the most diverse in linguistic terms. The Amazon lowlands are home to nine of Ecuador's eleven indigenous languages. The linguistic diversity of the lowlands mirrors the sociocultural and biological diversity characteristic of the country as a whole and of the Amazon basin in particular.[2]

---

1   In the Andean highlands: Highland Kichwa (Quechua); Tsa'fiki (Barbacoan); Awapit (Barbacoan). In the Pacific lowlands: Sia Pedee (Chocoan); Cha'palaa (Barbacoan). In the Amazon lowlands: Amazonian Kichwa (Quechua); A'ingae (unclassified); Paikoka-Baicoca (Western Tukanoan); Wao tededo (unclassified); Kayap (Zaparoan); Achuar chicham (Jivaroan); Shuar-Shiwiar chicham (Jivaroan).
2   Ecuador is considered one of the richest countries in terms of biodiversity and endemic species. Ten percent of the world's animal and vegetal species live in a small area of 256,370 square kilometers corresponding to 0.17% of the Earth's surface (Mittermeier 1988).

DOI: 10.111647/OBP.0032.07.

There is no agreement on the specific number of speakers of indigenous languages in Ecuador. This is due to the lack of transparent and updated sociolinguistic data. The size of Ecuador's indigenous population is clearly a political issue both for the government and indigenous peoples. The Confederation of Indigenous Nationalities of Ecuador (CONAIE), the largest indigenous organisation in the country, states that indigenous people represented one third (4,052,150) of the country's population (12,156,608) registered in 2001. In turn, the Council of Development of the Nationalities and Peoples of Ecuador (CONDENPE), the governmental agency of Indian affairs, maintains that Ecuador's indigenous people represent only 11 percent (1,103,957) of the national population (López & García 2009: 590). Moreover, the last census (2010) established that only 7 percent (1,018,176) of Ecuador's population is of indigenous descent (INEC 2010). However, the way in which censuses have been conducted so far is less than clear and the resulting data is often biased when it comes to indigenous peoples and communities. Today, an indigenous population of 2,000,000 is a reasonable estimate. Still, caution is needed because ethnic population—i.e. people self-claiming to be indigenous—is not equivalent to speaking population—i.e. people speaking one of the eleven indigenous languages. In such a case, the ratio between both populations depends on the ethnic group. Thus, the Cofán ethnic population is rather close to the population of speakers of A'ingae, the Cofán ethnic language, even if the rate of bilingualism among them is high; on the contrary, speakers of Kayapɔ, the Zapara ethnic language, count only 5 elders, representing scarcely 4% of the ethnic population (115), all of which speaks Amazonian Kichwa (Andrade 2001: 7).

The widespread use of Spanish in urban and rural areas, the labour migration of indigenous people to the cities and the partial success of bilingual education programmes have been determining factors in the decreasing vitality of indigenous languages. According to the UNESCO classification of endangerment (Moseley 2010), all of Ecuador's indigenous languages are in one way or another endangered and two have become extinct since the mid-seventies, Andoa and Tetete.[3]

---

3   Those critically endangered include Sia Pedee (Chocoan) and Zaparo (Zaparoan); the group of severely endangered languages is comprised of Paikoka-Baicoca (Western Tukanoan), Shiwiar (Jivaroan), Awapit (Barbacoan) as well as the highland varieties of Kichwa spoken in the provinces of Cañar, Azuay and Loja. Languages with a lesser degree of endangerment are A'ingae (unclassified), Achuar (Jivaroan), Shuar (Jivaroan), Tsa'fiki (Barbacoan), Cha'palaa (Barbacoan), and other highland and lowland varieties of

The classification of indigenous languages should be taken with caution because it is based mostly on estimates from census data. Only recently sociolinguistic surveys are being conducted among speakers of indigenous languages in order to determine their population with accuracy. Two of these languages are Tsa'fiki and Awapit. In both cases the data show tendencies different from those presented above (Gómez Rendón 2010a and 2011). Thus, Tsa'fiki should be considered a severely endangered language instead of a definitely endangered one, while Awapit is best classified as a critically endangered language rather than a severely endangered one in UNESCO's terms. Indeed, not even the indigenous languages with the largest population of speakers (Kichwa and Shuar) can be considered safe. On the other hand, one of these languages, Kichwa, has become so widespread in the Amazon lowlands that an increasing number of speakers of other minority languages are shifting to Kichwa. Similarly, Wao tededo, considered only vulnerable by UNESCO, is at present the most potentially endangered of all indigenous languages in the eastern lowlands because of labour migration and oil extraction activities within Wao ethnic territory. Moreover, this territory, which is part of an important wildlife reserve, Yasuní National Park, is home to the uncontacted peoples Taromenani and Tagaeri (Cabodevilla 2009).

Indigenous languages have become visible to the Ecuadorian Spanish-speaking society only in the last few decades thanks to the successful positioning of the indigenous movement since the mid 1980s and the principles of plurinationality and interculturality established by the 2008 Constitution. And yet, their use in public domains and education and their inter-generational transmission have not improved correspondingly. Ecuador remains a largely monolingual state and policy makers are more concerned with how to assimilate indigenous minorities into mainstream society and less with how to promote cultural and linguistic diversity as part of the country's ethnic composition.

The Constitution passed in 2008 establishes Spanish as the official language of the country while recognising Kichwa and Shuar as official languages of intercultural communication and the other indigenous languages as official in their respective ethnic territories. The Constitution requires that the State promote intercultural communication in indigenous languages and give indigenous peoples all the means necessary to develop

---

Kichwa. Wao tededo, the ethnic language of the Waorani group, is considered vulnerable, i.e. the least endangered of all.

an education system in their own language and with their own cultural contents. There has been some progress in intercultural bilingual education in the last two decades but there is still a long way to go. The appropriateness of the intercultural bilingual approach to indigenous education is now under discussion because a large portion of the ethnic population is still illiterate and the reading and writing of indigenous languages outside schools is minimal.

Indigenous languages and literacy: a tenuous relationship

Nowadays, each of Ecuador's indigenous languages has its own alphabet and orthography (Haboud 2009: 354).[4] Of course, these alphabets are not used by speakers of indigenous languages on an everyday basis. Except for Kichwa and Shuar, all other indigenous languages are written only in schools of the intercultural bilingual education system. Accordingly, textbooks and official documents in indigenous languages have very reduced readerships. This is explained firstly by the small number of indigenous speakers who can read and write in their native languages, and secondly by the type of language used in writing, full of coined expressions and neologisms that obscure the message.

The entry of Ecuador's indigenous languages into literacy is rather late as it took place only in the second half of the twentieth century. The only exception is Kichwa, a native language with a writing tradition dating back to the first missionaries who made use of it for evangelisation purposes in the early colonial period. They prepared grammars, dictionaries and religious texts including collections of prayers and catechisms.[5] Of course, all these texts were mainly intended for Spanish-speaking students of the language and not for the formal learning of grammar by Kichwa native speakers. These native speakers learnt to read and write in their language

---

4 This holds true even for the now extinct language Shimigae (Zaparoan), the ethnic language of the Andoa people, which was documented with its last speaker by the author in 2009. The outcome was a basic bilingual dictionary and a grammar for use in the re-introduction of the native language in Andoan schools (Gómez Rendón 2010b).

5 The first grammar of Kichwa was written by Domingo de Santo Tomás and published in Valladolid in 1564. The grammar was used for the teaching of the Inca language to priests and novices but also to Spanish-speaking civil servants who would deal with Kichwa communities (Cerrón-Palomino 1995: VII–LXVI).

only in the last decades of the twentieth century through bilingual education programmes. As for the other indigenous languages, their use in written form is even more recent. The first dictionary of Shuar (Jivaroan) appeared only in 1929 (Peñaherrera de Costales and Costales 2006: 181) and was prepared only for priests working in the Apostolic Vicariate of Mendez to learn the language for evangelisation ends.

The arrival of missionaries of the Summer Institute of Linguistics (SIL) in 1948 became a landmark in the literacy of Ecuador's indigenous languages. Based on the teaching of the Bible, their missionary work required a translation in the indigenous languages of the peoples they wanted to convert. Thus, their first efforts were devoted to carefully studying indigenous languages and giving them a writing system that could be easily used for reading and writing by missionaries and native speakers. SIL missionaries used the same Roman alphabet of the official language, with several diacritical marks to convey phonetic specificities. With some amendments introduced in the 1990s and 2000s, these alphabets are still used today in the intercultural bilingual education system.

The normativisation introduced by SIL missionaries had positive effects on creating a literacy tradition that survives in Ecuador to date. Literacy in indigenous languages was envisioned mainly for native speakers compared to the literacy tradition introduced by priests. But the work of SIL missionaries was not exempt from criticism: for one thing, the indoctrination in Western values and concepts destroyed native systems of beliefs and social interaction; for another, the use of literacy in indigenous languages was too often limited to religious contents and disregarded culturally significant material. Also, with a view to producing ready-made alphabets in order to begin with their evangelisation work, SIL missionaries set aside important dialectal differences that later on became a matter of contention among indigenous peoples, particularly once they became politically and culturally empowered in the last decades of the twentieth century (Stoll 2002).

Many other important advances in the literacy of indigenous languages took place during the second half of the twentieth century, particularly among the Kichwa-speaking communities. A model of literacy development was designed and self-managed by speech communities. In the early 1940s Dolores Cacuango, a female Kichwa activist, created a network of schools with the support of several urban women and local indigenous leaders; the schools were run by indigenous teachers who used the native language and promoted the indigenous culture and the defense of the ethnic territory. This experience is considered seminal for the development of today's intercultural bilingual education model. Similar literacy projects were carried out in the sixties and seventies in Bolívar (Simiatug) and Cotopaxi (Zumbahua and Chucchilán) with self-management or support from religious orders (Conejo 2008: 66–67). Other innovative experiences included the so-called radio schools (Escuelas Radiofónicas Populares) which broadcast for Kichwa speakers in the central highlands and for Shuar speakers in the eastern slopes. The remaining indigenous languages did not have literacy programs until the late 1980s.

The eighties was a decade of progress in the self-organisation of indigenous peoples in Ecuador. They strengthened their political stance and became visible and influential in the political arena (Sánchez-Parga 2010: 86). At that time, CONAIE, the largest indigenous organisation grouping representatives from all native peoples of the country, submitted an education proposal to the government which resulted in the creation of the National Director's Office of Intercultural Bilingual Education (DINEIB) in November 1988. Also, by an agreement between the Ministry of Education and DINEIB, the latter began to work on indigenous languages in order to conduct linguistic and pedagogic research for the preparation of teaching materials and training of bilingual teachers. Until February 2009, a few months after its twentieth anniversary, DINEIB operated as a financially and politically autonomous educational agency. At present, its status within the reformed educational system is still unclear. While nobody questions the importance of bilingual education as a mechanism for enforcing interculturality and plurinationality, the effectiveness of its administrative and organisational aspects has been criticised.

The outcomes of twenty years of intercultural education are not unimportant. By 2007, DINEIB ran 2,833 educational centres including primary and secondary schools as well as pedagogical and technical colleges, with 130,348 students and 8,355 bilingual teachers working in the highlands, the Pacific and Amazon lowlands and the Galapagos Islands (Conejo 2008: 79). Since 1993, all educational centers run by DINEIB have followed the Model of Intercultural Bilingual Education System (Conejo 2010) amended according to the last developments in curriculum planning and design by the Ministry of Education. Numerous teaching materials in book and digital formats have been produced since 1989, although the number of these materials is much larger for Kichwa and

Shuar than for the other languages, for some of which there are no updated teaching aids available, except those produced by private initiative. Also, there has been substantial progress in the normativisation of indigenous languages through a consensus-based definition of spelling in order to facilitate the teaching and learning of indigenous languages without the interference of the official language. Still, the changes in the spelling of indigenous languages continue to be a matter of contention, especially for those languages with an important dialectal variation such as Kichwa. In this respect, the process of identity politics led by indigenous peoples since the 1990s has in turn strengthened the linguistic identity of speech communities. In this context, the recent changes in the spelling system of Kichwa in 2008 have been strongly criticised by many highland communities, with the resulting rejection of teaching aids printed with the new spelling and the migration of school children to Spanish-speaking schools.

But these are not the biggest problems of intercultural bilingual education. The most serious obstacle to overcome is threefold: first, increasing retention and dropout rates in primary schools; second, the lack of a sound methodology and the poor training of bilingual teachers; and last but not least, the widely attested facts that literacy in indigenous languages occurs only in bilingual schools and "bilingual" students do not make any practical use of their native languages in writing beyond the classroom.

In sum, two decades of intercultural bilingual education have not resulted in a prolific and productive use of indigenous languages, neither in community contexts nor in public domains. Moreover, indigenous languages continue to be predominantly oral because their written use is limited and this limitation is most probably caused by the difficulties involved in writing due to changing spellings and the overuse of neologisms far from everyday natural speech.[6] And yet, this failure is, in my opinion, not imputable to intercultural bilingual education but to the unsatisfactory implementation of the model. Such implementation has disregarded the century-long oral tradition of indigenous languages and cultures and made all the efforts to bring them into literacy without any

---

6   Recent research supervised by the author found that writing in Spanish too is a problem for children attending intercultural bilingual schools. They cannot coordinate sentences properly and make themselves understood in Spanish. This means that the model of intercultural bilingual education as implemented so far has not succeeded in attaining proficiency in the official language (Contreras 2010).

consideration of their functionality. From this perspective, the fact that indigenous languages in Ecuador remain predominantly oral and alien to literacy should not be seen pessimistically. Orality must be integrated to intercultural bilingual education as a point of departure for literacy and the most important source of traditional culture and everyday knowledge.

Bringing orality to the foreground: new approaches in indigenous education and culture

Every human language has its roots in speech, and orality is speech by definition. Literacy is only a byproduct of culture and a medium for representing speech visually for recording and archiving purposes. Children learn languages first by listening while their first output is almost always oral. Literacy becomes part of their language only through formal schooling. Too often we forget this truism, perhaps because our visual culture leads us to assume that written signs are the essence of language. However, if literacy seems for us connatural to language, it is not the case for other societies, especially if they have been only lately exposed to written language. If such is the case of Ecuador's indigenous languages, then any educational model that makes use of them must bring orality to the foreground.

The above statement should not, however, be interpreted as if indigenous languages are not capable of becoming literate; the living proof of it are the hundreds of indigenous languages in the five continents which lacked a writing system before the twentieth century and now are widely used in written form. And yet, orality continues to be their main mode of communication and the most natural context in which their cultural heritage is passed on to new generations. It is therefore misleading to assume that the gap between orality and literacy in indigenous languages can be bridged in any successful way in only a few decades.

Bilingual education models should not forget the history of literacy behind their languages. In the case of bilingual education in Ecuador, the history of literacy in the official language (Spanish) boasts hundreds of years while the same history in indigenous languages is in its infancy. But, most importantly, bilingual education models should not disregard what is perhaps the most influential of all factors, i.e. diglossia. Indeed, the official language in Ecuador has a privileged sociopolitical position *vis-à-vis* indigenous languages, and while the official language is used in private and public domains alike, indigenous languages are restricted to family and community. The pressure exerted by the official language on speakers of indigenous languages has led to Hispanicisation (speakers' shift to Spanish by abandoning their mother tongue) or language mixing (speakers' use of Spanish lexical and grammatical borrowings with structural changes in the native languages).

Against this backdrop of historical, political and social factors that influence literacy in indigenous languages, it is self-evident that orality is not a drawback in bilingual education, i.e. something that formal schooling must eradicate once and for all. On the contrary, orality should be the point of departure for literacy in indigenous languages, and the best way to show and perform orality is through ears and eyes and always in contexts of cultural significance.

Language labs: a meeting point for orality and literacy

While the idea of a language laboratory is not new for the teaching and learning of international languages such as English or French, the same idea brought to the field of indigenous languages becomes a challenge to the racist prejudice that views indigenous languages as "dialects" undeserving the investment of time and money. Behind this prejudice is the surviving romantic idea that indigenous languages are by definition "traditional", something of the "past" that cannot be the object of "modern" technologies. Unfortunately, this view is held by most Spanish monolingual citizens in the cities. In this context, the concept of a language laboratory was launched as an innovative though risky proposal for intercultural bilingual education in 2008. Being an expensive project, it was designed first only for Kichwa, the largest language in terms of the number of speakers but also the one with enough digital material available.

The conditions in which the project was launched were particularly favourable as the language laboratory became, since then, part of the so-called "millennium schools". Millennium schools are educational centres located in poor, mostly rural areas that so far have been neglected in education. Their facilities and architectonic design are related to an innovative pedagogical model which takes into account the local ethnographic characteristics; facilities include so-called "thematic" classrooms for the teaching of specific subjects and are equipped with cutting-edge technologies. However, the most important and innovative characteristics of millennium schools have to do with their pedagogical model. Given their experimental nature, millennium schools follow a participative educational project that takes into consideration the cultural, social and economic elements of their areas of influence and seek to establish a democratic and equitable culture in economic, social, ethnic and gender terms. In sum, millennium schools make use of an innovative educational model alongside proper facilities, teaching aids, well-trained teachers, and the active participation of parents and community.

The Kichwa language laboratory implemented in millennium schools has four components as described in the following:

1) Linguistic software for interlinearised transcription of audiovisual files, lexical databases, morphological parsing and acoustic analysis; the software was intended mainly for the training of Kichwa language teachers in grammatical analysis and lexicography, but also for them to collect and edit pieces of oral tradition

2) Digital resources that include a multimedia dictionary for children, a touch screen board, thematic maps and different accessories in Kichwa; these resources were intended for school children as a first introduction to Information and Communication Technologies (ICTs)

3) A library of digital books in Kichwa and footage of different size, from films to video clips about various aspects of Kichwa culture, including traditional music and songs in the language, a collection of myths and legends told by storytellers from different Kichwa communities, and several didactic videos for teaching specific skills such as weaving, sculpting, painting and carving

4) Digital teaching aids including interactive textbooks and workbooks as well as tests for evaluation of the learning progress

The language laboratory was designed as an interactive space for Kichwa-speaking children to use their native language orally and in writing. Children would be exposed to speech events in their own cultural contexts through the use of multimedia. The principle behind this design is that audiovisual material, if properly used, provides contextualised language learning in culturally significant situations through listening and watching.

The same principle is applied to the learning of grammar. In this case, children are not passive learners of rules but assimilate such rules from listening to examples of spontaneous speech that they can play once and again.

At the moment Kichwa language laboratories have been implemented in all millennium schools located in Kichwa-speaking areas and also in a few Spanish-speaking schools, as Kichwa is a language of intercultural communication and all Ecuadorian citizens ought to know it at least rudimentarily. While several problems have arisen in the experimental stage, which have to do with the insufficient training of teachers in the proper use of high-tech equipment and software, the project is still underway and is expected to extend to other indigenous languages.

Intangible cultural heritage: the coming of age of a concept and its use in identity politics and indigenous education

The concept of "intangible cultural heritage" is not as old as that of "cultural heritage". However, in the early 1990s, discussions began about the so-called intangible aspects of culture, and UNESCO finally adopted a Convention for the Safeguarding of Intangible Cultural Heritage in 2003 (UNESCO 2003).[7] In Ecuador the implementation of the 2003 Convention has resulted in an official recognition of the heritage status of indigenous cultures, so far reduced to folklore in state policies.

Ecuador became a state party to UNESCO in 1975 through the acceptance of the World Heritage Convention. Since then, it has participated actively in the safeguarding of architectonic heritage. This resulted in the inscription of Quito's historic centre in the world heritage list and the foundation of a specific agency devoted to safeguarding Ecuador's cultural heritage (Instituto Nacional de Patrimonio Cultural). This heritage included two sets of elements: 1) architectonic pieces and sites in urban areas; and 2) archaeological monuments and sites, most of them associated with the Inca presence in Ecuador. Because indigenous peoples do not have monuments

---

7   The Convention defines intangible cultural heritage as "the practices, representations, expressions, knowledge, skills—as well as the instruments, objects, artifacts and cultural spaces associated therewith—that communities, groups and, in some cases, individuals recognise as part of their cultural heritage" (UNESCO 2003).

or sites of the same sort as those found in cities and archeological complexes, their material cultures, let alone other less "tangible" expressions, were never considered a form of cultural heritage.

The acceptance and ratification of the Convention by Ecuador in 2008 represented a dramatic turn in cultural politics, with great influence on the public management of cultures, those of the urban Spanish-speaking population and those of the indigenous peoples all over the country. Moreover, the acceptance of the Convention is a landmark in the recognition and promotion of cultural rights as it is congruent with the principles of interculturality and plurinationality claimed by the Ecuadorian state.

The instrumentality of intangible cultural heritage has been seriously considered by governmental agencies and is being evaluated by indigenous peoples as a mechanism to enforce their collective rights before the state. This is made possible because intangible cultural heritage is linked to other fields of public policy such as health care and education, and because the concept of cultural heritage includes a network of multifarious expressions and prescribes the understanding of cultures in their own specificities. In the case of Ecuador's indigenous peoples, such specificities are necessarily determined by their languages and the oral character of their tradition.

Immediately after the acceptance by Ecuador of the Convention for the Safeguarding of Intangible Cultural Heritage, a nation-wide project was conducted for the identification of intangible heritage among indigenous peoples. Another nation-wide project was started in 2010 to produce a more detailed, ethnographic and multimedia inventory of intangible heritage in order to take specific measures of safeguarding. The outcomes of both projects so far have been significant and include 1) a database containing hundreds of intangible elements of Ecuador's indigenous cultures, with their basic description, identification data and georeference; and 2) audiovisual material of different expressions of intangible heritage, including festivals, crafts, medicinal knowledge, oral tradition, and so forth. Together with the safeguarding of previously identified heritage in danger of extinction, one step towards the empowering of communities in the management of their own heritages is to mobilise the outcomes of inventory and documentation for educational purposes and the revitalisation of indigenous cultures. When it comes to this point, however, the State and the indigenous peoples have to come to terms with delicate issues concerning intellectual property rights, the return of outcomes to the communities, the practical accessibility of such outcomes, and the management of audiovisual material. This task is not easy in the absence of a law on intellectual property rights, a code of conduct and a general framework that enables the direct participation of indigenous peoples in decision making about their own heritage.

Ethical and legal issues in orality and literacy concerning indigenous peoples

The folklorisation of indigenous cultures in Ecuador by governmental and non-governmental agencies has prevented their consideration as objects of legal protection. By considering intangible culture as people's heritage, the 2003 Convention paves the way for their protection as property with all of the related rights.

The fact that intangible cultural heritage often lacks physical support and is mainly collective in nature makes it more sensitive to illegal appropriation by outsiders. Let us consider in this respect the case of oral tradition. Under the cover term "oral tradition" indigenous peoples include not only what we usually name as myths, legends, songs, and the like, but also other, perhaps "more practical" knowledge that is enacted and transmitted orally as the knowledge related to biodiversity, forest conservation or natural medicine. Now, to the extent that language is the main vehicle of intangible cultural heritage, any knowledge, practice or expression is coded in language and hence part of oral tradition. Therefore, protecting intangible cultural heritage as collective property implies protecting language firstly through revitalisation, in case it is being threatened by a dominant official language; secondly, through its active and creative use in the education of indigenous peoples; and thirdly, through the construction of a legal framework that enables speakers of indigenous languages and owners of intangible cultural heritage to control the dissemination of any linguistically coded element of their cultural heritage.

Three sensitive issues have been identified in relation to the management of orality and literacy of indigenous languages and intangible cultural heritage in Ecuador. The first issue addresses the tension between collective and individual rights in terms of property. While property in general may be owned by a person or by a group of people, intangible cultural heritage is always owned by a group even if it can be preserved and transmitted individually. Take, for example, the case of the last medicine-man of an indigenous Amazonian group: as an individual he possesses a rich knowledge about the use of plants and herbs, but his knowledge is not his personal property but the product of the collective experience of his people in their century-long coexistence with the tropical forest; the fact that in principle the last medicine-man can transmit his medicinal knowledge through language practically to anybody poses a problem to the distribution of such knowledge and the property of it in relation to his people.

The second controversial issue has to do with the use of language as part of intangible cultural heritage. In recent years the video and audio recording of speech events has become the standard of language documentation (Himmelmann 2006: 9). Over a hundred documentation projects all over the world have been generously supported by research institutes and non-governmental organisations. Documenting linguistic diversity seeks to preserve languages for posterity in a context in which half of today's 6,500 languages will be extinct in the next hundred years (Crystal 1996; Bradley and Bradley 2002). The idea of preserving linguistic diversity as an expression of our species is certainly valuable, but it is less so when the great majority of documentation projects are focused on archiving only, i.e. without a view to mobilising outcomes for the survival of languages and cultures. The ethical question posed here is about the use of archiving when not accompanied by practical efforts to eradicate the threats of language extinction. The use of language documentation is clear when viewed from the perspective of linguists and anthropologists or even from that of governmental agencies concerned with positioning the nation-state in the multicultural market. However, when seen through the lens of speakers themselves, the relevance and practicality of language documentation becomes blurred by other more important matters concerning their physical and cultural survival. It is certain that obtaining informed consent of the speech community rather than individuals and sharing views of documentation with a larger audience can help to get the meaning through, but still it is not enough. Language detached from culture and culture detached from physical survival lack sense for speakers as human beings. In countries like Ecuador, the socioeconomic situation forces indigenous speakers to abandon their native language for Spanish and leave their cultural heritage behind. It is simply a matter of survival. From this perspective, the only way to carry out documentation as part of intangible cultural heritage and education is to assume an integral view of linguistic rights as part of economic, social and cultural rights.

The third issue involves the distribution of documentation outcomes. If documentation outcomes must serve the social, economic and cultural promotion of indigenous peoples, then indigenous peoples must be the first users of those outcomes. On these grounds, it is essential to discuss with speech communities more practical ways to make outcomes of documentation easily accessible to them. It is useless, for example, to simply return digital copies of audiovisual material to the communities if they do not have electricity or DVD players or personal computers. Similarly useless is the return of copies of scientific papers, books or dissertations in languages unknown to speakers or about topics of little use to the promotion of their languages in education. From this perspective, a valuable descriptive grammar about an endangered language written in English with all the linguistic jargon becomes useless for teachers of a bilingual education school who are in urgent need of a basic grammar *in* their own language. The same criterion is valid for any documentation of cultural heritage, which is supposed to serve the community first and foremost. The other side of the documentation outcomes involves outsiders, i.e. individuals or groups who are neither speakers of indigenous languages nor owners of their cultural heritage. In Ecuador, outsiders can be city dwellers who speak the dominant language or governmental agencies of culture, but also national and international scholars who make use of documentation outcomes for writing their papers and scientific reports. Here the question is not the level of accessibility for outsiders but rather who establishes those levels and if they are established *jointly* with the community. It is also a question of where the outcomes are deposited and what the privacy policy of the depository is. It has often been the case that products of language documentation are deposited with individuals instead of institutions. In other cases depository institutions are abroad and therefore not easily accessible to communities that want to make use of documentation outcomes. Moreover, accessibility levels have too often been determined without consultation with indigenous leaders, thereby disregarding the collective character of cultural heritage.

The above discussion does not cover all the issues concerning the management of documentation outcomes but suffices to give us an idea of how thorny the questions may be, in particular when customary practices involve property rights from a purely economic and individual perspective. Therefore, a legal framework is necessary which addresses these issues, in particular the individual/collective nature of rights in relation to intangible cultural heritage and language, the accessibility of outcomes for insiders and the limits of accessibility for outsiders.

Orality and literacy in indigenous cultures: perspectives and challenges

It is often stated that the world's linguistic diversity will disappear in the next centuries as a result of globalisation (Nettle and Romaine 2000; Mufwene 2002). This admonitory statement, however, disregards a fact widely attested in all continents: the ethnic resurgence of groups so far silent or invisible which now choose to speak up and claim their own identity and culture. This ethnic resurgence is supported in many cases by developments in national and international legislation. Today, cultural and linguistic diversity is as important as biological diversity because it is seen as the outcome of thousands of years of species adaptation. Cultural and linguistic diversity is therefore an asset for societies in the world's multicultural market and explains why states that previously claimed cultural and linguistic homogeneity now promote cultural and linguistic rights. This is the case of Ecuador and of many other Latin American countries, in which the state has assumed a role of protector of rights and promoter of cultural diversity in a context of ethnic resurgence and along with a new politics of identity.

Because most ethnic groups have been excluded for centuries from the sociopolitical developments of nation-states, their cultures have remained influenced by the dominant culture and yet outside the formal schooling system. In this context, the entry of ethnic groups to literacy took place only in the second half of the twentieth century. In Ecuador, after twenty years of intercultural bilingual education, indigenous languages and cultures remain predominantly oral. But instead of being an obstacle to the revitalisation of indigenous languages and cultures, orality represents an unending source of knowledge that should be profited from. The question is two-fold: on the one hand, how to promote orality without denying indigenous speakers access to literacy; on the other, how to protect intangible cultural heritage of indigenous peoples in ways that prevent its folklorisation and commoditisation by outsiders. The answer to both questions lies in the proposals discussed here. One is a new model of intercultural bilingual education that takes orality as a point of departure for the development of literacy and makes extensive use of available ICTs in order to provide students with socially relevant material and culturally contextualised learning. The other is the safeguarding of intangible cultural heritage as part of the enforcement of social, economic and cultural rights of ethnic groups, respecting their property rights from a collective rather than individual perspective, providing them with easy access to documentation outcomes, and consulting them throughout the process of identification, inventory and documentation of their languages and cultural heritages so as to avoid paternalistic practices. Policy makers, governmental agencies, non-governmental organisations, research institutes and scholars must realise that talk about endangered languages and cultures goes beyond languages and cultures and involves human beings. Only this realisation shall lead us to recognise the multifaceted nature of endangered languages and cultures and to make effective contributions to their survival rather than remain silent witnesses of their extinction.

References

Andrade Pallares, Carlos, *Kwatupama Sapara. Palabra Zápara. Obra maestro del patrimonio oral e inmaterial de la humanidad (UNESCO)* (Quito: Prodepine, Anazppa, 2001).

Bradley, David, and Maya Bradley, eds., *Language Maintenance for Endangered Langauges: An Active Approach* (London: Routledge Curzon Press, 2002).

Cabodevilla, Miguel Ángel, *El exterminio de los pueblos ocultos* (Quito: CICAME, 2009).

Cerrón-Palomino, Rodolfo, 'El Nebrija Indiano', in *Estudio Introductorio a la Gramática o Arte de la Lengua General de los Indios de los Reynos del Perú* (Cuzco: Centro de Estudios Regionales Andinos Bartolomé de las Casas, 1995), pp. VII–LXVI.

Conejo, Alberto, 'Educación Intercultural Bilingüe en Ecuador. La propuesta y su proceso', *Revista Alteridad*, 5 (2008), 64–82.

—, *Modelo del Sistema de Educación Culutral Bilingüe. Actualización 2010. Colección Runakay* (Quito: Ministerio de Educación del Ecuador & DINEIB, 2010).

Contreras Ponce, Enrique, *Análisis de las relaciones entre oralidad y escritura en textos producidos por maestros y alumnos de la escuela Cacique Jumandy del Pueblo Kichwa Rukullakta, provincia del Napo* (unpublished master's thesis, Universidad Andina Simón Bolívar, 2010).

Crystal, David, *Language Death* (Cambridge: Cambridge University Press, 1996).

Gómez Rendón, Jorge, 'El patrimonio lingüístico del Ecuador. Desafío del siglo XXI', *INPC Revista del Patrimonio Cultural del Ecuador*, 1 (2009), 7–24.

—, *Vitalidad de la lengua Tsa'fiki en las siete comunidades Tsáchilas de la Provincia de Santo Domingo* (unpublished report, Instituto Nacional de Patrimonio Cultural, 2010a).

—, *Andoa-Kichwa Shimiyuk-Panka* (Quito: Fundación Aurelia Figueras, 2010b).

—, *Vitalidad de la lengua Awapit en comunidades seleccionadas de las Provincias de Esmeraldas, Carchi e Imbabura* (unpublished report, Instituto Nacional de Patrimonio Cultural, 2011).

Haboud, Marleen, 'Ecuador en el Pacífico', in *Atlas Lingüístico de los Pueblos Indígenas de América Latina*, ed. by Inge Sichra (Ecuador: Imprenta Mariscal, 2009), pp. 652–659.

Himmelmann, Nikolaus P., 'Language Documentation: What Is It and What Is It Good For?', in *Essentials of Language Documentation*, ed. by Nikolaus P. Himmelmann and Ulrike Mosel (Berlin: Mouton de Gruyter, 2006), pp. 1–30.

Nettle, Daniel and Suzanne Romaine, *Vanishing Voices: The Extinction of the World's Languages* (Oxford: Oxford University Press, 2000).

Mittermeier, Russel A., 'Primate diversity and the tropical forest', in *Biodiversity*, ed. by O. Wilson (Washington DC: National Academy Press, 1988), 145–154.

Moseley, Christopher, ed., *Atlas of the World's Languages in Danger* (Paris: UNESCO Publishing, 2010). Third Edition.: <www.unesco.org/culture/en/endangeredlanguages/atlas> [Accessed 24 October 2012].

Mufwene, Salikoko, 'Colonization, Globalization and the Future of Languages in the Twenty-first Century', *International Journal on Multicultural Societies*, 4 (2) (2002), 162–193.

Peñaherrera de Costales, Piedad and Alfredo Costales, *La Nación Shuar*, vol. 1 (Quito: Editorial Abya Yala. 2006).

Sánchez-Parga, José, *El movimiento indígena ecuatoriano* (Quito: Editorial Abya Yala, 2010).

Stoll, David, *¿Pescadores de hombres o fundadores de imperio?* (2002) <http://www.nodulo.org/bib/stoll/ilv.htm> [Accessed 24 October 2012].

Online Sources

Instituto Nacional de Estadística y Censo, *Resultados del Censo (INEC) 2010* <www.inec.gob.ec/cpv/index.php?option=com_wrapper&view=wrapper&Itemid=49&lang=es>

UNESCO-United Nations Educational, Scientific and Cultural Organization, *Convention for the Safeguarding of Intangible Cultural Heritage* (2003) <http://www.unesco.org/culture/ich/index.php?lg=en&pg=00006>

7. From Shrine to Stage: A Personal Account of the Challenges of Archiving the Tejaji Ballad of Rajasthan

Madan Meena

The story of Tejaji

Tejaji is a snake deity widely revered by the agrarian community throughout Rajasthan, parts of Madhya Pradesh, and Gujarat. According to popular belief, he was born in the village of Kharnal of Nagaur district (historically known as Marwar state) of Rajasthan during the tenth century AD[1] probably to a Jat (community) family. The story goes that he was married very early as an infant and was unaware of the fact until he grew to adolescence. One day, goaded by his sister-in-law, he learnt about his married status and so resolved to visit his wife's village and bring her home. Before doing so he first went to his sister's village to bring her back and then left to collect his wife. He encountered many bad omens as he started his journey but continued undeterred. It is this interesting journey to his wife's village and his encounter with the snake to whom he gives his life that form the content of the sung Tejaji Ballad.

The Tejaji Ballad

The Tejaji Ballad occupies an important part of the sung oral tradition in Rajasthan.[2] The singers are non-professionals who have built up expertise

---

1 See Thakur Deshraj (2002: 305).
2 The tradition of Tejaji singing has traveled to the adjoining states of Madhya Pradesh and

DOI: 10.111647/OBP.0032.08.

through years of continuous performances at Tejaji shrines. The tradition is not caste- or community-specific: the singers and devotees come from all sections of society, small Tejaji shrines exist in every village and different fairs and festivals mark the importance of the deity. During the Tejaji fair, the performance of the ballad is the most important of all the rituals performed at the shrine. A separate style of Tejaji performance also exists in the region in the form of *khel*[3] enacted on stage as a serial drama over several nights, but this has almost died out.

In its original form, men come together at night to sing the Tejaji Ballad during the monsoon months. This period used to be spread over two months but increasingly the performances only begin close to the main festival of Teja-Dashmi which marks the end of the season.

The aim of the performance of the ballad is to induce the spirit of Tejaji to enter the priest (*Bhopa*)[4] so that he can exorcise snake poison from man or beast. The possibility of encountering snakes is highest during the monsoon when the ballad is sung. The narration of the ballad supports a strong belief that whoever ties a thread in the name of Tejaji will survive the snakebite. Traditionally, the singers are called upon to perform whenever an urgent case of snakebite arises or when an offering is made for the fulfillment of a wish. The ballad symbolises reverence to the deity for life. Thus the performers, performance and the *Bhopa* are strictly related to the shrine of Tejaji and these cannot be separated.

Traditionally, the singing of the Tejaji Ballad takes place at the village shrine with the singers and instrumental players sitting on the ground facing each other in a circle. In the majority of modern performances, two men sing the ballad accompanied by a few others. In one village, people remembered groups of up to fifty men facing each other. One initiates the basic lines of the ballad and the other repeats them. The accompanying musical instruments used are *dholak*,[5] *algoza*,[6] *manjira*[7] and also hand clapping (Figure 1). The recordings hosted by the World Oral Literature Project, and made in

---

Gujarat through continuous migrations of the Raika (shepherd) community in search of pastoral lands. The Raikas are devotees of Tejaji and they sing the ballad in great reverence.

3   These are types of dramas enacted in villages at nights during the festive time. Also called *nautanki* in north Rajasthan.

4   A priest of the shrine who is also in charge of it. He possesses spirits of the deities and gives alms to villagers to aid with their problems.

5   A barred-shaped double-headed drum played with hands on both sides.

6   A double-flute producing a drone effect, played with fingers on both flutes simultaneously.

7   Brass cymbals played with two hands in continuous rhythm.

Thikarda village, were done in this traditional style with these instruments. There are very few men left who can play the *algoza* and it is a dying craft.

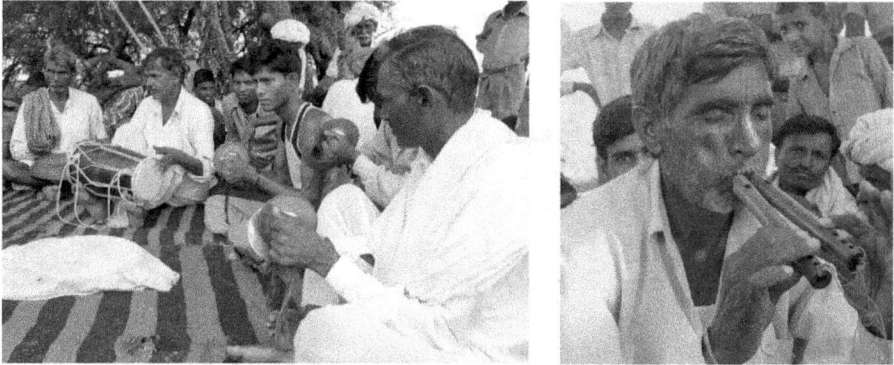

Figures 1 and 2.   Accompanying instrumental players. The *algoza* is being played in Figure 2. The player is using a continuous stream of breath and does not need to punctuate the music with breaths. Photograph by Madan Meena, 2010.

Iconography

The Tejaji Ballad illustrates the sacrificial deed of Tejaji. It establishes his ideal human character in keeping his promise. During the narrative of the ballad, the character Tejaji loses his life in obedience to his promise to a snake whilst on a journey to bring his wife home. The snake bites him on the tongue as this is the only place still unbloodied after his heroic adventures. The ballad is infused with local references to make it more relevant to the present-day life of the people, for example the singers mention a flood in the Kali Sind river when Tejaji goes on a pilgrimage to Badrinath shrine. Geographically, Badrinath lies in the Himalayas (north India), while Kali Sind is a local river in the Hadoti region.[8]

The popular image of Tejaji is as a warrior sitting on a mare holding a spear in his hand and with the snake climbing up to bite him (see Figure 3). This image is found in calendars, cassette covers, shrine paintings, and in stone reliefs.[9] In the village of Sureli in Tonk district, the *Bhopa* imitates the

---

8   The region derives its name from Hada Rajputs who settled in the region in the twelfth century and dominated the area for several centuries thereafter. At one time, the Hada-ruled state of Bundi encompassed the present-day districts of Baran, Bundi, Kota, and Jhalawar. See James Tod (2002: 355). A map of the Hadoti region is available at <http://bit.ly/Z3wjey>.

9   The earlier relief sculptures, found in old shrines of Tejaji (e.g. the Tejaji shrine in the

incident of the snake biting his tongue on the occasion of the Teja-Dashmi festival,[10] at which the crowds go wild. I was able to video-record this moment for the archives but was not able to get a good sound recording because of extraneous noises and the general chaos.

A day prior to the eve of Teja-Dashmi, the *Bhopa* moves in a procession sitting on a mare holding the snake round his neck. The next day he allows the snake to bite him on his tongue. For a moment after the snake bites he appears to lose consciousness but is brought back to life by the crowd singing Tejaji songs. At the end of the festival, in the evening, the snake is released into its hole. The *Bhopa* who performs this is quite old and his successors may not be able to follow it in future. This performance is a unique enactment in the whole of Rajasthan.

Figure 3.   Iconic image of Tejaji represented in a painting. Painted by Gopal Soni, Bundi. Photograph by Madan Meena, 2010.

Figure 4.   A *Bhopa* of the Tejaji Shrine in Sureli, Tonk, imitating a snake-bite with a real Cobra on the occasion of Teja-Dashmi festival. Photograph by Madan Meena, 2010.

---

village of Dugari in Bundi district), depict his image in a more abstract way. In later images (e.g. the Tejaji shrine at Balchandpara in Bundi), the detail is refined. These images of Tejaji are washed regularly and decorated with colorful foil and sindoor (vermillion) (Bharucha, 2003, for this and all other glossary terms) on *dasse*, i.e. on the tenth day of every Hindu Bhadwa month.

10   The festival of Teja-Dashmi falls on tenth day of Bhadwa Hindu month i.e. in September. The day is marked with celebrations at Tejaji's shrine, the cutting of the threads, and a number of important fairs. People fast on that day (they eat once in the evening), offer *prasad* (offerings) and hoist flags at the shrines.

The project

During the current project, the full twenty hours of the Tejaji Ballad were recorded, transcribed into the local Hadoti language, and translated into Hindi and English as part of fieldwork supported by the World Oral Literature Project. The final objective was to publish a book along with an audio DVD, which were freely distributed these among the singers, villagers, schools and libraries in the area. This will help in preserving the ballad for future generations.

The main singers in my recordings are of the Mali[11] community of Thikarda[12] village (Figure 5) situated near Bundi town in the Hadoti region. The recordings were made during the monsoon season in 2010 at the local Tejaji shine outside the village, and at night to avoid external disturbances. Though the ballad can be sung at any part of the day when the need arises to invoke the spirit of Tejaji, it is usually sung at night-long *jagarans*.[13] The singers and the instrumental players were mostly in their late fifties and sixties. The young generation was generally absent from the *jagarans,* as with easy availability of other entertainment options they are not interested in these traditional performances. Recording the complete ballad took six night-long sessions spread over two months. The musicians cannot sing on consecutive nights as they are too exhausted and it was always a challenge to fix up the next recording session and to collect the same group of performers.

---

11   The Mali community are commonly recognised as gardeners in the whole of north India. Two main sub-castes of Mali exist in Rajasthan according to the interviews with the Thikarda Mali: those who are involved in the cultivation of flowers for the shrines and temples are called Phool-Mali, and those involved in agricultural practices and vegetable cultivation are called the Gheevar Mali. The Mali of Thikarda village are Gheevar Mali who have small land holdings (one acre on average) on which they grow vegetables and supply them to nearby Bundi town.

12   The village Thikarda is situated ten kilometers from Bundi across the hills to the north. At one time it was a part of Bundi state. Today it has a population of some 5,000 people, mainly of the Mali community, followed by Kumhars (potters), Meghwals and Rajputs.

13   *Jagarans* are all-night singing sessions where devotees gather at the shrine to listen to the musicians who sing devotional songs. The purpose of the Jagrans is to invoke the deity.

Figure 5   Tejaji singers of the Mali community at village Thikarda. Photograph
by Madan Meena, 2010.

Alongside Thikarda village, recordings were made in some twenty-four
other villages in the Hadoti region and adjoining areas in order to get a
sense of the variations and nuances in styles.

Challenges of recording

In many villages, the singing is so endangered that it only happened
because I was commissioning it. The singers are now limiting its
performance to around the main festival of Teja-Dashmi. The quality of
the recordings was affected by the fact that instruments needed repair
and vocalists were out of practice.

The performers do not think of themselves as individuals and do not like
to be singled out by name. They see themselves as being interchangeable
and as part of a performance. This was a challenge for recording, as
I wanted the same musicians each time to maintain continuity for
archiving purposes but they did not see this as important.

I was trying to record a full version of a twenty-hour Tejaji Ballad
spread over several nights in as genuine a context as possible. Thikarda
village is now the only village in which singers are able to perform the
whole ballad. Increasingly, sections are sung when a *jagaran* is called.
As snakebites are completely unpredictable it was difficult to be there

when a genuine performance was happening, to try to capture and understand the difference in intensity of performance between one called when a life was at stake, and one called for archiving purposes. I was at a shrine once when a buffalo was brought with a snake bite and it died in front of me.

On occasions when someone else had organised the performance I had little influence over the time and venue and, if there was heavy rain, the performance would be cancelled at the last minute. If the performance was carried out, the spirit might not come for several hours and it was hard to keep the musicians going and for myself to stay awake through the recording session. The most successful recording sessions in terms of sound quality were those which I commissioned myself although the authenticity was compromised.

I recorded on thirty-six nights out of sixty in August and September 2010. For a genuine performance, a *jagaran* has to be called and a feast thrown.[14] This involves ghee and *puja*[15] material as well as *beedis*[16] and endless cups of tea for the musicians and the audience. At one recording, I provided refreshments for one hundred people (Figure 6). This was not the norm, however, and the problem was to attract an audience. In such performances a local audience is necessary as they are the real patrons. They boost the performers by responding to the music and this interaction becomes part of the performance. The singer and musicians would sing for thirty minutes to an hour with intermediate breaks for smoking, chewing tobacco and drinking tea. The performance was exhausting and therefore the instrument players took turns, but these supporting players tended to fall asleep after being tired from agriculture work. This wasted valuable time on many occasions as I was trying to keep the same performers throughout the recordings for the integrity of the archive. At the end of a session, they would have to be shaken awake.

---

14   All the recordings were carried out at Tejaji's shrines by organising *jagarans* and feasts in honour of the deity. This was in order to maintain originality and the context of the tradition.

15   Offering to the deity.

16   Locally made cigarette by stuffing tobacco into a leaf pipe.

Figure 6.   Thikarda singers having a feast of *daal-baati*[17] and *churma*[18] after the *jagaran*. Photograph by Madan Meena, 2010.

The performance is traditionally carried out until the spirit of Tejaji enters the *Bhopa*. However, the spirit often would not come until 4:00am and the singers had to keep going in turns until it happened. Once the *Bhopa's* body is possessed by the spirit of the deity, his voice and behaviour change and he acts as the deity himself, and addresses the problems of the devotees. At one village called Nayagaon near Bundi, because of the many hours that had passed and the spirit had not come, all the musicians fell asleep and I had to give up for the night.

Another challenge was to collect the musicians in the first place. If a *jagaran* is called they have to come, but I would always have to wait two or three hours each time to gather them at the shrine despite all prior contacts and invitations having been made. If it rained heavily, the event would be cancelled or moved inside where recording became impossible because of sound resonance and *beedi* smoke.

To record at one of the villages inhabited by the Kanjar community, notorious for its illegal activities and crime, I had to take a police escort. Everyone in the village was drunk, including the instrumental players. But the performance turned out to be fabulous and was participated in by women dancers, which I had not seen before (Figure 7). The performers

---

17   Rajasthani village dish of wheat balls made and cooked in a cow-dung fire and eaten broken up and mixed with ghee and daal.

18   Sweetened mixture of crushed *baati* served with *daal-baati*.

moved in a colourful procession, which went round the village the whole night finally culminating in a frenzied gathering at the Tejaji shrine in the morning. During the performance it was not just one *Bhopa*, but many who all took turns to be possessed by local deities. Some of the performers had passed out by the morning from their excesses.

Figure 7.   Kanjar women dancing to the tune of the Tejaji Ballad. Photograph by Madan Meena, 2010.

Having worked with the more sober Thikarda singers last year, I was able to gain their confidence. It is not traditional to pay them individually but to donate something for the shrine. In return for the six recording sessions, the shrine has new paintings and a cement floor outside, on which villagers can perform under a tree. The village has decided that it wants money towards a roof for the new cement floor and I have promised Rs. 20,000.[19]

At the end of the recordings during the Teja-Dashmi *mela* (local fair) I called the performers and honoured each with a flower garland and a *dhoti*.[20] They appeared to be satisfied, but with other groups it was different. Some groups assumed that I was going to make money out of the recordings and therefore demanded a high fee and travel expenses. Others wanted me to publish cassettes and CDs for them in return for playing. Very few could

---

19   Indian Rupee.
20   Loin cloth worn by men.

understand the concept of the recordings being for academic and archiving purposes.

During recording sessions at many places, the singers could not be motivated to sing without the installation of a sound system. They have become so accustomed to microphones that the pitch and volume at which they sing has considerably reduced. They feel uncomfortable singing without the microphones. Impractically, they especially like to listen to themselves during the performance by tilting one of the loudspeakers towards themselves. With the use of microphones and amplifiers, the singers do not have to exert themselves. The empathy between the singer and the instrumental players is lost. An external person controls the blend and volume of the ballad by monitoring and adjusting the input signal levels whereas in the absence of any amplifying equipment, the singers and players have to listen to each other and adjust their volume accordingly.

For authentic recordings, the loudspeakers and amplifiers were a big hurdle (Figures 8 and 9). They generate lots of echo and extra sound in the background. Also the spontaneity is not present in such microphone-supported performances. In such situations, I cancelled my recordings so as not to disturb the *jagaran* called by the villagers.

Figures 8 and 9.   Singers holding the microphone, and an amplifier installed on a cart. Photograph by Madan Meena, 2010.

From shrine to stage

Over the years, a shift in tradition has lead to stage performances. One reason for this is the popularity of religious Hindu *bhajan*[21] performances on stage. The Tejaji singers are evolving their style accordingly. They are

21   Generic term for devotional song.

moving out from the confines of the community to larger prominence, seeking audiences despite the challenge of influences from outside. This type of performance was not worth recording for the purposes of my project but it is a very important trend and will lead to the loss of genuine performances and opportunities to record in the future.

The repertoire is losing its strength on stage. When the group sings the Tejaji Ballad at a village shrine, it is sung in consecutive mode, and the story progresses in linear manner. On stage, multiple groups participate and the time duration is short, thus only a popular part of the ballad is sung. The audience is very diverse, and the aspect of entertainment is more important than belief. Thus the singers, dancers and electronic equipment and instruments dramatise the performance: the objective is shifting from honouring the deity to gathering accolades of the audience.

One reason for the evolution of a stage style is the desire of the middle class development lobby to provide a platform for the dying rural traditions. Musicians are invited to urban or even international platforms and encouraged to devise a short programme that will fit into the constraints of a planned set-piece entertainment. Under the name of "Hadoti Culture", the audience is treated to an overblown, overdressed Bollywood-style parody of the Tejaji tradition with even a female singer backing up the storyteller. There is always a prancing horse dancer and usually a man twirling an umbrella. The audience, which probably does not understand the language of the singing, is introduced only to the visual elements. For generations the traditions of the Tejaji Ballad have survived in the environment of socio-religious beliefs and customs. Only time will tell how far the stage will carry them and in which direction.

Thus from this perspective of rapid changes to the Tejaji Ballad, the authentic traditional style is losing ground. Most of the performers are aged and the new generation is not interested in learning the tradition. The modern values of education do not support the belief in Tejaji. At the present time, no one who has been to school likes to tie a thread in the name of Tejaji if bitten by a snake. He or she will immediately rush to the hospital to get the anti-venom treatment. This is obviously a good development but it means that the old oral tradition is so under threat that my recording may be the last occasion on which the ballad is sung in its entirety.

The challenges of recording the Tejaji Ballad for archiving purposes, and for offering the ballad in a pure form to the people of Hadoti, have been many and varied but, for the most part, successfully met and personally, it has been a most rewarding experience. As proposed, the twenty hours of the ballad with Thikarda singers was recorded successfully in its original style keeping in mind the technical archival standards. This project has opened doors to further recordings in other villages as people themselves have welcomed me to record their groups. They are beginning to understand the value of archiving such traditions. Once the singers are recorded they are very keen to get a copy of it immediately after the recording. With the aid of computers and bluetooth devices they download it to their cellphone handsets and mp3 players. I hope that this will help in popularising this tradition if not as a belief system then at least as a singing tradition. Thus, after this project the future effort will be to record and archive as many Tejaji Ballad singing groups as come forward, and to produce on-demand audio DVDs for them. The urgency to record the different styles of the ballad prevalent in different parts of Rajasthan has been very apparent during the project. I plan to concentrate on archiving them with support from outside or independently.

The audio-video and written records of this project will serve as a snapshot of cultural heritage for the future, but will also constitute a fossilised archive of a constantly changing important Hadoti oral tradition. Hopefully this will serve as a model for archiving similar traditions prevalent in Rajasthan, which are also on the verge of extinction. Apart from archiving it, the publication of the book and audio DVD will help in promoting its value and importance amongst the younger generation.

References

Bharucha, Rustom, *Rajasthan, An Oral History: Conversations with Komal Kothari* (New Delhi: Penguin Books, 2003).

Deshraj, Thakur, *Jat Ithihas* (Delhi: [n. pub.] 2002).

Government of India, *Survey of India Maps* (India [n.p.]: Government of India, 1998).

Meena, Madan, *Tejaji Gatha* (Kota, Rajasthan: Kota Heritage Society, 2012).

Tod, James, *Annals & Antiquities of Rajasthan*, 2 vols (India: Rupa & Co, 2002).

Online Sources

World Oral Literature Project, *Madan Meena: Tejaji Gatha collection* <www.oralliterature.org/collections/mmeena001.html>

8. Mongghul Ha Clan Oral History Documentation

Ha Mingzong 哈明宗, *Ha Mingzhu* 哈明珠
and C. K. Stuart[1]

以父母之心为心，天下无不友之兄弟；

以祖宗之心为心，天下无不睦之族人。

If you take the wishes of your parents to heart, there won't be any unfriendly brothers;

If you take the wishes of your ancestors to heart, there won't be any inharmonious clansmen.[2]

The Mongghul

The Mongghul (Monguor, Tu) are one of several groups of people who are collectively classified as the Tu nationality in China, where they are one of fifty-six officially recognised ethnic groups. "Mongghul" is a phonetic transcription of the self-appellation of certain groups of Tu living in Huzhu Tu Autonomous County, Ledu County, and Datong Hui and Tu Autonomous County in Qinghai Province; and in Tianzhu Tibetan Autonomous County, Gansu Province. Certain Mongghul elders refer to themselves as Qighaan "White" Mongghul and refer to Mongols as Hara "Black" Mongghul. Some Tibetans refer to them as "Hor", while Chinese

---

1 We thank Veronikia Zikmundová, Gerald Roche, and Limusishiden for helpful comments on this chapter.
2 Excerpt from the Old Chronicle of the Hawan Mongghul Ha Clan. The verse was originally written by Emperor Qianlong (1711–1799) in the literary work 'Shengjinfu 盛京赋'.

DOI: 10.111647/OBP.0032.09

and Hui used "Tu ren" and "Tu min", both meaning "Tu people" (Chen et al. 2005: 1), before the official designation "Tu" was created after the establishment of the People's Republic of China (PRC).

In 2011, many classified as Tu born around 1980 or later, refer to themselves as "Tu" as a result of the near universal education system in Chinese, the official designation of Tu, being monolingual in Chinese, the possession of identity cards specifying their ethnicity as Tu, and their ethnicity stated as "Tu" in matters of official administration.

There are a number of early works on the Monguor. These include Mostaert and de Smedt (1929, 1930, 1931), Schröder (1952/1953, 1959, 1964, 1970), and Schram (2006 [1954–1961]). More recently, the diversity of the Tu nationality has been demonstrated by studies and collections related to the Tu living in Tongren County, Huangnan Tibetan Autonomous Prefecture, Qinghai Province (Janhunen et al. 2006, Fried 2009, Fried 2010); and Shaowa Tu Autonomous Township, Zhuoni (Janhunen et al. 2007). In addition there have been studies focusing on the Huzhu and Tianzhu Tu (Ha and Stuart 2006, 2008, Ha 2007, Faehndrich 2007); and the Mangghuer of Minhe Hui and Tu Autonomous County, Qinghai Province (Slater 2003).

Authorship in Chinese by PRC writers on the Tu, with the Tu imagined as a single homogeneous ethnicity, has generally focused on history and origins using historical Chinese-language texts, with few in-depth local studies utilising community elders' knowledge. This tendency to write Tu history using written texts that are often unclear partly explains multiple, competing interpretations. These writings generally make a connection with the Tuyuhun and Xianbei, who are represented as Tu ancestors (Lü 2002, Hu 2010), or arguments are presented that the Tu are descended from Mongol troops who came to the current Qinghai-Gansu area during the time of the Mongol conquests, the Shatuo,[3] and Han Chinese (Li 2004, Li and Li 2005). In contrast, the oral history documentation project of the Mongghul Ha Clan[4] prioritised the value of local oral history as told by community elders with the goal of making it available worldwide to anyone with an interest, including future generations of Tu people.

It is important to note that migrations, intermingling, and identity transformation of nationalities have been frequent in the Qinghai-Gansu frontier region, making it challenging to claim that the Tu ethnicity is unambiguously derived from a single ancestral group. Disputes and the

---

3 The Shatuo were a local section of the Ancient Turks (Janhunen, 2006).
4 Clan refers here to a group sharing a common surname and a common genealogy or chronicle.

generation of academic papers regarding Monguor origins are likely to robustly continue. This is due in part to the complicated genesis of the ethnicity of the Tu, and the manner in which the Tu category was created in new China. The dearth of material utilising the knowledge of living illiterate elders and such materials as local clan chronicles emphasises how contemporary Chinese historiography has so often neglected knowledge passed down from generation to generation. Such materials can provide vital information and allow for a more nuanced view of ethnic history.

In terms of Monguor clan histories, Louis Schram's work on the Liancheng Lu Clan (2006 [1954–1961]),[5] and Li and Li's research (2008) are noteworthy in using clan chronicles to examine the history of the ethnicity. As Nietupski notes, Schram "provides a record of ethnic Monguor clan lineage from its own perspective and gives detail about the *tusi*[6] office and heritage" (2006: 35). Schram's work suggests that the Lu Clan is of Mongol imperial origin. Li and Li's book (2008), which makes frequent use of Schram, combines local chronicles with historical Chinese language materials providing further particulars about Mongghul clan origins, especially the two Mongghul Li clans, one of which they claim is of Mongol origin and one of Shatuo origin.

Recording and preserving what living Mongghul elders know of their own history is an urgent task. They are the last group able to repeat generationally transmitted knowledge about clan origins, migration routes, settlement areas, important local figures, and clan genealogy, as well as modes of livelihood, relationships local people had with government, and cultural expression. In addition, they have a rich orally transmitted repertoire of songs, folktales, proverbs, and knowledge of various cultural expressions that are of great importance in illuminating the history of cultural origins, interrelationships, and language studies. The exigency of recording such information is further emphasised by the realisation that very little of this knowledge is being recorded, the heritage-bearers are rapidly passing away, and that the younger generations possess little of this knowledge.

In recognition of these issues and the value placed on living elders' knowledge, we chose the Ha Clan (two authors' clan) to study, and make such knowledge publicly available.[7]

---

5   Liancheng Town is located in contemporary Yongdeng County, Gansu Province.

6   Tusi = Chinese-appointed or inherited-post local officials; "hereditary local chief" (Nietupski 2006: 30, 33).

7   The Mongghul Ha Clan consists of the West Ha Clan (Mongghul Ha Clan members from or who moved away from Xihajia (West Ha Clan) Village), and East Ha Clan members, who are from or previously were from Donghajia (East Ha Clan) Village, Huzhu County, Qinghai.

The Mongghul Ha Clan is not mentioned as a Mongghul clan in any written historical sources that we have identified. Is this due to ignorance of such historical sources, or the claim by many contemporary West Ha Clan members that "we were originally not Mongghul" refers to historical fact? To answer these questions and gain further insight into Ha Clan history, the project focused on oral history and family chronicles that survived New China's chaotic early history.

The Mongghul Ha Clan chronicle

Family chronicles found in China often provide valuable information unrecorded in official history writings. The Hawan Ha Clan chronicle consists of two parts written in Chinese. The first is the Old Chronicle composed in the seventeenth year of the Guangxu Reign (1875–1908) of the late Qing Dynasty.[8] The New Chronicle was composed in 1992 and 1993 as a continuation of the Old Chronicle.[9] Two sections of the Old Chronicle have survived. The first is a six-page preface and the second is a forty-eight page chronological listing of clan members' biographies that record birth and death dates, place of interments, and very brief life narratives. This information allows descendants to know where and when visits should be paid to their ancestors' graveyards.

Originally a genealogical registry of the clan's ancestors existed called *zongnan* in the local Chinese dialect, or *zong'an* in Modern Standard Chinese. It was, according to clan elders, a large piece of cloth that covered nearly one wall of a room. The clan ancestors' names were written and their portraits sketched on the *zongnan*, which co-existed with family chronicles. The Ha Clan *zongnan*, the oldest known record of the clan and the only copy that existed, was destroyed in 1958 during Pochu mixin yundong "Destroy Superstition Movement".[10] The New Chronicle records the following with regard to the *zongnan*: "We formerly had a roll of white silk cloth that was more than three meters long and 1.6 meters wide called *zongnan*. It featured our ancestors' sketches. Among them the most prominent was that of Yinxi Taiye".[11] Another

---

8   Preface of the Ha Clan's unpublished Old Chronicle (1892).
9   Preface of the Ha Clan's unpublished New Chronicle (1993).
10 Campaigns engendered by Posijiu "Smash the Four Olds" (old customs, culture, habits, and ideas) began in 1966 and resulted in widespread destruction of family chronicles in China.
11 Yinxi refers to the tradition of the emperor bestowing titles and ranks to his subjects on the basis of their immediate ancestors having been high-ranking officials and having honorably served the court. "Taiye" literally refers to one's great-grandfather; it is also an honorific title for an ancestor.

section of the New Chronicle gives generation names that help clan members understand relationships to other clan members. Such relationships are of fundamental significance in Mongghul social structure, where social position in the local community is determined by the generation one belongs to. For example, where one should sit at a wedding ritual where guests are seated according to their generation, the order of the families one visits during the Chinese lunar New Year period, terms of address used for family members in the homes visited, and the order in which liquor is offered, are determined by generation and age. This unified system of generation names differentiates generations by means of a word in every clan member's name. For example, in the names of two of the chapter's authors "Ha" is the surname and "Ming" indicates their generation (which is the same). Only the third character in this case is unique, "zong" and "zhu". This unified system is used both in the West and East Ha Clans (Ha 2007).

Figure 1.   Old Chronicle of the Mongghul Ha Clan in Hawan Village. Photograph by Ha Mingzong, 2009.

Mongghul Ha Clan origin

People with the surname Ha are found among Hui, Mongolian, Tu, and Han ethnicities.[12] The Mongghul Ha Clan *zongnan's* destruction was a serious blow to the study of its origins; the New Chronicle that was created about thirty-five years later is largely based on elders' recollections. Regarding clan origins, the New Chronicle preface reads:

> In terms of Ha Clan history, the clan originated from Zhuji Street in today's Nanjing City. In 1376, two brothers moved to Huangzhong and then soon moved to Halazhigou in Huzhu County. The elder brother settled on the west side of the river, and hence the origin of the West Ha Clan. The younger brother settled on the east side, and hence the origin of the East Ha Clan.[13]

The accounts of Qinghai natives having originated from Nanjing are many among both Mongghul and Han and, perhaps, the account of Mongghul Nanjing origins was created relatively recently (Schram 2006 [1954]: 125, 164). Such an account is absent from the surviving pages of the Old Chronicle. In any case, all the Ha Clan consultants interviewed during this project stated that their ancestors originated in Nanjing.

The *Digital Version of Ha Clan History*[14] suggests that people with the surname Ha in China descended from two brothers—Hala Buding and Hala Buda—who were of Karluk/Geluolu (Halalu) origin and were military commanders of the Oirat Khaan Esen Taiji. Their surname, Ha Baocheng writes, is a phonetic transcription of the first syllable of their own non-Chinese names (personal communication, 2010).

In 1452, the two brothers moved to central China—Zhongyuan—where they became renowned military generals of the Ming (1368–1644) court. The surname Ha became first known in China during this period.

The son of the elder brother, Hala Buding, later moved from Nanjing to Hejian—in today's Hebei Province—and became the most prominent military general in Hejian following his father's death. The younger brother, Hala Buda, remained in Nanjing and became a prominent military officer.

---

12 Ha Baocheng, an independent Hui scholar living in Beijing, has compiled A Digital Version of Ha Clan History, which he shared with Ha Mingzong. Most of the material from this collection is available from his website in Online Sources. Ha Baocheng contends that Hui with the surname Ha originated from the Muslim Khanate of Bukhara.

13 Preface of the Ha Clan's unpublished New Chronicle (1993). Original text: 溯述哈氏之由来，族根系南京珠玑巷。大明洪武九年（公元1376年）迁徙湟中（古称西宁地区，未岁，迁居互助县哈拉直沟，哥住河西，俗称西哈家，弟住河东，俗称东哈家。

14 See Online Sources

During this period the Ha Clan divided into two parts: one moved north and lived in Hejian and the other stayed in Nanjing. Ha Baocheng also wrote in personal communication to Ha Mingzong that most of those with the surname Ha in today's Qinghai and Gansu provinces migrated to these locations from Nanjing during the Ming Dynasty.

It should be noted that the New Chronicle states that Ha Clan ancestors moved from Nanjing to Qinghai in 1376. Ha Baocheng's research suggests the Hala brothers came first to Nanjing in 1452, which he states is the approximate time of Ha Clan origins in China. There is thus obvious discrepancy in Ha Baocheng's findings and the New Chronicle. Ha Baocheng also suggests that most Mongghul Ha Clan members in today's Qinghai and Gansu were originally Han and later were classified as Tu when the Chinese government began establishing minority autonomous regions in the 1950s and the local government in today's Huzhu needed more people in the Tu ethnic category in order to establish an autonomous county in Huzhu.

The two villages with the most Ha Clan members in Huzhu County are Xihajia Village where, in 2009, there were seventy-eight families (about 380 people) of whom only two families were from another clan. The second village is Donghajia where, in 2009, there were forty families (approximately 220 people) of whom three families were from other clans. Xihajia Village residents with the surname Ha were all classified as Han, while Donghajia Village residents with the surname Ha were all classified as Tu. Ha Clan members in Hawan Village are also registered as Tu.

Migration from Huzhu to Tianzhu

From the late nineteenth century when the Gansu frontier was ruled by Ma Qi (1869–1931) and his son, Ma Bufang (1903–1975), Xihajia was under the jurisdiction of Xining Fu, or "Xining Administration".

Part of the Xihajia Ha Clan moved to Hawan in three phases from 1918 to 1942. Others moved to Yetu and Dakeshidan villages in Tiantang Town, Xidatan Township; and Anyuan Town in Tianzhu County.[15] The digital collection of information related to these migrations, based on interviews with local clan elders, was a major project focus. The initial migration of part of the Xihajia Village Ha Clan occurred in 1918 when Ha Nangsuo

---

15   Data collected by Ha Mingzong during his fieldtrips.

moved his family to Hawan as the result of Ma Qi's efforts to increase the size of his army by forcibly drafting men into his service.[16] According to Chen (2009: 13), salaries and supplies for his army were originally provided by the Gansu government, but after Ma Qi became increasingly autonomous, government support ended and he began collecting money and property from the citizenry. Later, when Ma Bufang (known locally as Tu Huangdi "Local King") came to power, drafting men into the army intensified and taxes increased (Li and Li 2005: 302–304).

According to stories told by elders interviewed, Ma Bufang ordered Mongghul women to stop wearing headdresses and other traditional clothing. Those who refused were vilified and sometimes beaten. Elders said they dared not speak Mongghul within earshot of Ma Bufang soldiers, for fear of punishment. Consultants also said that Ma Bufang conscripted local carpenters, blacksmiths, and masons because of their specialised skills. For example, the interviewee Ha Baode (b. 1939) mentioned that his father, a carpenter fearful of being captured by Ma Bufang's soldiers, frequently stayed away from home working in such areas as the contemporary Tianzhu County, where Ma Bufang's influence was less great. When he had accumulated enough money to build a new house in Hawan, he moved his family there. Elders also stated boys and men aged fifteen to fifty were forced into Ma Bufang's army; such conscriptions were implemented two or three times annually, leaving only old people, women, and children in the village. It was under such circumstances that many Hawan Ha Clan members' ancestors along with many other people fled to Tianzhu and also why many Tianzhu residents speak the Qinghai Chinese dialect today.

---

16 Schram (2006 [1954–1961]: 306–07) describes *nangsuo* as an institution originally created by the Ming court in Huangzhong for local lama chiefs to carry out tasks such as "the granting of a territory, the fixing of a yearly tribute, the recognition of the chieftainship of the lama who had brought in the tribe, and of the heritability of that chieftainship".

Figure 2. Interview with Gazangshiji (front row, third from left, b. 1932) and Wushisan (second from right, b. 1947) at Gazangshiji's home in Dakeshidan Village, Tiantang, Tianzhu, Gansu Province, China, in August, 2009. Photograph by Ha Mingzong, 2009.

Figure 3. Interview with Ha Baode (right, b. 1939) and his grandson Ha Mingshan (middle, b. 1997) at their home in Hawan Village in September, 2009. Photograph by Ha Mingzong, 2009.

Figure 4.   Interview with Layeshiji (1946–2007) and Lan Jiraqog (b. 1927) at Lan Jiraqog's home in Hawan Village in February 2005. Photograph by Ha Mingzong, 2005.

Figure 5.   Interview with Ha Shenglin (1942–2009) at his home, Hawan Village, in February, 2005. Photograph by Ha Mingzong, 2005.

The current situation of the Mongghul Ha Clan

As discussed earlier, Mongghul Ha Clan members who are originally from Huzhu County live in Xihajia and Donghajia villages in Danma Town, Huzhu County. In Tianzhu Tibetan Autonomous County, Ha Clan members dwell in Yetu, Hawan, and Dakeshidan villages of Tiantang Town, Anyuan Town, Xidatan Township, and Huazangsi Town.

Communication between the modern-day Gansu and Qinghai branches of the Ha Clan has been intermittent over the years. Several Hawan elders have visited their ancestral home in Xihajia and the clan cemetery. Apart from a decreasing number of elders, few Ha Clan members understand that less than a century ago, a clan branch moved to Hawan. When asked to explain this lack of communication, the answer was typically, "We don't know anybody there".

Several elders in Xihajia Village speak Mongghul while all others speak only the local Chinese dialect. The linguistic situation is very different in Donghajia Village where nearly everyone speaks Mongghul. Only a fifteen minute walk across a riverbed and a road that leads to Xining separates the two villages, raising the issue of why such a difference in villagers' knowledge of Mongghul developed. Local accounts suggest that a Xihajia villager known as Hajia Xiansheng "Ha Clan Master" was educated in the Chinese language, thought highly of the importance of Chinese, and encouraged fellow villagers to speak and learn this language. Other reasons remain unclear for this startling difference in language abilities between the two nearby villages of the same clan.

Historically, the inconvenience of travel made the distances separating various Ha Clan settlements difficult and thus cross-community visits were impractical and communication sporadic. Over the years, differences between these settlements have developed. For example, all Xihajia residents are registered as Han, speak the local Chinese dialect, and follow local Chinese marriage and burial ceremonies, whereas people in Donghajia are registered as Tu, speak Mongghul, cremate their dead, and sing Mongghul songs at weddings. Ha Clan people in Hawan, though of Xihajia descent, speak Mongghul, while the generation born around 1990 have varying ability in understanding and speaking Mongghul. Most Hawan Mongghul, in 2011, spoke Chinese more often than Mongghul, no longer wore Mongghul clothing, nor sang in Mongghul, and generally felt there was little difference between Tu and local Han.

Figure 6.   Xihajia Village: Home-village of the Mongghul Ha Clan in Hawan Village. Photograph by Ha Mingzong, 2009.

Figure 7.   Hawan Village. Ha Mingzong and Ha Mingzhu's home village. Photograph by Ha Mingzong, 2008.

For the entire West Ha Clan, the Mongghul language is maintained only in Hawan Village. The number of Mongghul speakers is decreasing rapidly in Hawan because more children go to schools where the only language used is Chinese, villagers go to other areas for long periods of the year to work where Chinese is the *lingua franca,* and on account of an increasing number of marriages with Chinese and Tibetan women who do not speak Mongghul.

Project approaches

An inspiration for undertaking this project was the debate over the issue of Tu history. We felt that Mongghul elders had important information and we were determined to bring to life and permanently record their stories and thoughts as it often differs from texts focusing exclusively on written sources. We also felt a responsibility to future generations of Mongghul youth to provide a record of their ancestors' memories. Consequently, Ha Mingzong and Ha Mingzhu visited Mongghul Ha Clan members in Xihajia and Donghajia villages in Huzhu; Hawan, Yetu, and Dakeshidan villages and Huazangsi Town in Tianzhu; and Akesu in Xinjiang and made audio and video recordings of interviews. This information was easily copied onto DVDs and VCDs which, as Gerald Roche et al. comment, fit into "the video-disc (VCD) era of today" because almost every village family has a VCD or DVD player (2010: 154). Community elders were enthusiastic about the audio-video documentation of their family stories for posterity.

Local reactions

The project elicited different points of view among locals. Villagers from all the Ha Clan communities that we visited welcomed us: an expression of their code of hospitality. After explaining the purpose of our visit, elders encouraged us with comments on the importance of the preservation of family oral history. Elders understand that after they pass away, most of their cultural knowledge and memories will also vanish. Clan elders also thought highly of the idea of producing DVDs and VCDs from the interviews to supplement information in the clan chronicles.

In contrast, the younger generation was largely indifferent, though they were keenly interested in the recording equipment and the idea of "being on TV". We sensed considerable scepticism of the project's importance and practicality. For example, on one occasion as Ha Mingzong was interviewing an elder about family history, a man in his twenties joined us, took Ha Mingzong's notebook, looked at his notes, put the notebook down with a bored expression, and asked late in the interview what Ha Mingzong's purpose was in collecting such information. He added that such information did not enhance skills learnt at school and was not helpful in finding employment. When Ha Mingzong replied that he thought that cultural preservation was important, this man asked why Ha Mingzong, who was studying abroad, would choose to study his own people when he had the chance to learn things that could not be acquired at home and besides, he added, many local Mongghul would probably always know more about themselves than he would.

Ha Mingzong and Ha Mingzhu's family and relatives generally did not understand why they were involved in such projects that focused on an intensely impoverished past and present reality that many people spend a lifetime trying to escape. Such reactions and attitudes reflect a concern that activity should deliver a monetary reward quickly: cultural documentation is not seen as providing financial benefit.

Project outcome

Ha's *Mongghul Ha Clan Oral History* (2010) was based on oral interviews and contributes to the study of Mongghul history by presenting a digital, oral history of the Mongghul Ha Clan. Ha Clan elders surprised us by suggesting a possible origin of the Mongghul Ha Clan from Nanjing in south China. The project also resulted in a transcribed, translated, and glossed interview conducted with Ha Shenglin (Appendix 1) that gives information on family history, childhood, clan migration, and religious beliefs and thus has historical, ethnographic, and ethnolinguistic value, given the dearth of such content in both written and oral texts.

Selected interviews were transcribed using the Transcriber program that allows preservation and presentation of both the audio file and the transcription, allowing for the oral text to be presented simultaneously with the corresponding transcription. This permits readers to follow the exact transcription while listening to the recording. A screenshot of such transcriptions may be seen in Appendix 2.

DVDs and VCDs were produced from interviews and activities filmed, and given to community members, including the interviewees, who received not only their own interviews, but also interviews from other Ha

Clan villages. These compact discs hold both images and voices, preserving memories of people, places, and a certain time in history, providing clan members with heretofore unknown information, strengthening a sense of clan unity, and providing locally a unique record of Ha Clan members across Ha Clan communities. These were all major project goals.[17]

A participatory approach to cultural documentation was used, prioritising the value of local oral history as related by community elders, making it available worldwide to anyone interested and with an Internet connection. By digitally documenting and presenting the oral history of a relatively large Mongghul clan living across an extended area, new historical insights into Tu history became available. This is obvious in the death of Ha Shenglin. At present, no one in his immediate family knows the details of his father's and grandfathers' lives; information that was recorded by Ha Mingzong is now available.

The lives of contemporary Tu youth are increasingly influenced by images of a privileged life lived by China's elite and in the West, and modern global pop culture such as Korean soap operas that have been popularised through the ubiquity of television, compact video discs, and the Internet. There is extreme poverty in some of the most traditional Mongghul communities, evident through lack of access to basic health care and resources that would pay for such care, clothing that is plain and simple, and an education system that is dramatically inferior to that available in such urban centres as Xining and Lanzhou. Knowledge of oral history and Mongghul songs, wearing Mongghul clothing, and a profound knowledge of local Mongghul history do not give most Mongghul youth a sense of belonging to a glittery attractive global pop culture. It is the latter to which they aspire: to be able to dance, sing, and dress like pop icons, and enjoy an affluent life.

However, as the decades pass and people's lives continue to improve economically and become increasingly synonymous with global urban culture, future Mongghul generations may search for their roots in an effort to distinguish themselves from much of the rest of humanity. To conclude, we offer this account by Ha Mingzong:

> I was born and raised in Hawan Village, a Mongghul village, which was surrounded by Chinese speaking Han, Hui, and Tibetans. All villagers in Hawan speak Chinese and, in the late 1990s, all could also speak Mongghul.

---

17 Relevant recordings of Ha Clan oral history are available on the World Oral Literature Project website, Ha Mingzong: Mongghul Ha Clan Oral History (see Online Sources).

Villagers switched between languages when they talked to each other. I lived in the village during the first fifteen years of my life and never heard a fellow villager sing in Mongghul.

I attended schools where classes were taught in Chinese, and where Han, Hui, Tibetan, and Mongghul students and teachers all spoke Chinese. Raised in such an environment led me to believe there were no appreciable differences between local Chinese, Tibetans, and my Mongghul community, other than I spoke an additional language, since most local Tibetans in Tianzhu only spoke Chinese. It never occurred to me that there was a gap in our thinking and behaviour.

This attitude changed in 2002 when, at the age of sixteen, I enrolled in the ETP (English Training Program) at Qinghai Normal University, a programme initiated in 1997. I was the lone non-Tibetan in a class of students from Qinghai, Sichuan, Yunnan, Gansu, and the Tibet Autonomous Region. I quickly realised that I was different from my Tibetan classmates for they all spoke languages I did not understand. Some classmates thought I was a Han Chinese teenager who happened to speak Mongghul. I was singled out for a long time. A part of me felt proud that I was different, but I was not proud of knowing little about Mongghul culture. There were occasions when we were asked to sing traditional songs and I was put in an awkward situation because I could not sing any Mongghul songs, unlike my Tibetan friends, many of whom knew many traditional songs.

I then wished to know more about Mongghul culture. That was why I was very pleased when I was introduced to an older Mongghul folk researcher and started doing cultural preservation projects. I wanted to learn more about my culture in the process. And I did. I borrowed CDs and VCDs of recorded Mongghul folk songs and learned them. I also began digitally documenting Mongghul folklore from many Mongghul villages and distributing the materials back to the local communities, including my own, where such recordings sometimes brought tears to the eyes of old people who dearly appreciated them and the memories they resurrected after having been surrounded by pop music for years.

Based on my experience, it is important to know a great deal about Mongghul culture in order to be proud of being Mongghul, because this brings knowledge about what there is to be proud of, which leads to confidence in being Mongghul. Time spent studying Mongghul culture and history is solely up to the individual; it is not taught in any schools.

My experience in cultural preservation has allowed me to discover my people and, in so doing, I have more fully discovered myself: a road less travelled that has already taken me much farther than I ever expected.

Appendix 1: Transcription, Translation and Glossing

Location: Ha Shenglin's home, Hawan Village, Tiantang Township, Tianzhu Tibetan Autonomous County, Wuwei Region, Gansu Province, China

Date: 18 February 2005

Interviewer: Ha Mingzong (A)

Interviewee: Ha Shenglin (B)

1.   Family Members

(1)A:	*Uh,*	*aadee*[18]		*niudur*	*saa,*
	HES	granduncle		today	PRT

Bu	*qi-mu-la*		*nige*	*tangxaa-le-la*		*ire-wa.*
1s	2s-ACC-COM		one	chat-VBLZR-PURP		come-PERF

Uh, Granduncle, today I have come to have a chat with you.

(2)B:	*Sain-na.*
	Good-OBJ.NARR

Good.

---

18   *Aadee* may refer to a person's grandfather or any male from the grandfather's generation.

(3)A:	*Yaan*	*tangxaa-le-genii*		*ge-sa,*
	what	chat-VBLZR-SUBJ.FUT		QUOTE-COND

diijuu	*Haja*	*kun-ni*	*Lishi*[19]*-ni*
actually	Ha.Clan	people-GEN	history-ACC

nige	*tangxaa-le-la*	*ire-wa*	*bai.*
one	chat-VBLZR-PURP	come-PERF	PRT

What I am here to talk about is actually the history of Ha Clan people

(4)B:	*Au...au,*	*dui*	*dui*	*dui....*
	AGREE	right	right	right

Oh, right, right, right...

(5)A:	*qi-mu,*	*qi*	*qi-ni*	*nara-ni,*	*qi*	*nige*	*kile*	*bai.*
	2s-ACC	2s	2s-GEN	name-ACC	2s	one	say	PRT

Please, you, tell (me) your name.

(6)B:	*Mu-ni*	*nara*	*maa?*
	1s-GEN	name	QUEST

My name?

(7)A:	*Uh.*
	AGREE

Yes.

---

19 Chinese *lishi*历史= Mongghul *lorji* = Tibetan *lo rgyus.*

(8)B:	*Nara*	*si*	*diijuu,*	*uh...*	*qidar-la*		*hao,*[20]
	Name	COP	actually	HES	Chinese-INSTR		PRT

uh...	*yaan-na*		*bai,*	*Ha*	*Shenglin-na*	*bai.*
HES	what-OBJ.NARR		PRT	Ha	Shenglin-OBJ.NARR	PRT

Mongghul-la		*hao*	*dii*	*mu-ni*	*nara*	*si*
Mongghul-INSTR		PRT	then	1s-GEN	name	COP

Bu	*Uje-ya*	*yaan-na*		*saa?*
1s	See-VOL	what-OBJ.NARR		PRT.quest

Uh,	*ndaa*	*si,*	(interference...)
HES	me	COP	

Niangniang	*ndaa*	*bao-ki-ja*		*bai,*
Niangniang	me(ACC)	protect-VBLZR-OBJ.PERF		PRT

Bao'ai	*Wa*	*bai.*
Bao'ai	OBJ.COP	PRT

My name, actually in Chinese is Ha Shenglin and in Mongghul, it is, let me see, uh, what is it? Bao'ai, since Niangniang protected me.

---

20 From the local Qinghai Chinese dialect.

Appendix 2: Transcription and Translation

Synced transcription and translation of an interview (audio file) using Transcriber.

Appendix 3: Selected Transcriptions of People and Places

A

Akesu 阿克苏
Anyuan Town 安远镇

B

Beijing 北京

D

Dakeshidan 大科什旦
Danma Town 丹麻镇
Datong Hui and Tu Autonomous County 大通回族土族自治县
Donghajia Village 东哈家

E

Emperor Qianlong 乾隆

G

Gansu Province甘肃
Guangxu 光绪

H

Ha Baocheng 哈宝成
Ha Baode 哈宝德
Ha Mingshan 哈明山
Ha Nangsuo 哈囊索
Ha Shenglin 哈生林
Hajia Xiansheng (Ha Clan Master) 哈家先生
Hala Buda哈剌不达
Hala Buding哈剌不丁
Halalu 哈剌鲁
Halazhigou哈拉直沟
Han Chinese汉
Hawan Mongghul Ha Clan 哈湾

Hebei 河北
Hejian 河间
Huangnan Tibetan Autonomous Prefecture 黄南藏族自治州
Huangzhong 湟中
Huazangsi Town 华藏寺
Hui 回
Huzhu Tu Autonomous County 互助土族自治县

K

Karluk/Geluolu 葛逻禄

L

Ledu County 乐都县
Liancheng Lu Clan 连城 鲁

M

Ma Bufang 马步芳
Ma Qi 马麒
Ming court 明
Minhe Hui and Tu Autonomous County 民和回族土族自治县
Mongghul Li clan 李

N

Nanjing City 南京

P

Pochu mixin yundong (Destroy Superstition Movement) 破除迷信运动
Posijiu (Smash the Four Olds) 破四旧

Q

Qing 清
Qinghai Province 青海

S

Shaowa Tu Autonomous Township 勺哇土族自治乡
Sichuan 四川
Smash the Four Olds 破四旧

T

Tiantang Town 天堂镇
Tianzhu Tibetan Autonomous County天祝藏族自治县
Tibet Autonomous Region 西藏自治区
Tongren County 同仁县
Tu Huangdi 土皇帝 (local name for Ma Bufang "Local King")
Tu min (Tu people) 土民
Tu ren (Tu people) 土人
Tu 土
Tuyuhun 吐谷浑

W

Wushisan五十三

X

Xianbei 鲜卑
Xidatan Township 西大滩乡
Xihajia Village 西哈家
Xihajia 西哈家
Xining Fu (Xining Administration) 西宁府
Xinjiang 新疆

Y

Yetu 业土
Yinxi Taiye 荫袭太爷
Yinxi 荫袭
Yongdeng County 永登县
Yunnan 云南

Z

Zhongyuan 中原
Zhuji Street 珠玑巷
Zhuoni 卓尼
zongnan/ zong'an (genealogical registry) 宗案

References

Chen, Zhaojun and Xinghong Li et al., *Folktales of China's Minhe Mangghuer* (Muenchen: Lincom Europa, 2005).

Chen, Bingyuan 陈秉源, *Ma Bufang jiazu tongzhi qinghai sishi nian* 马步芳家族统治青海四十年, (Xining西宁: Qinghai renmin chubanshe青海人民出版社) [*Ma Bufang Family's Forty Year Reign in Qinghai* (Xining: Qinghai People's Press, 2007)]

Faehndrich, Burgel R. M., *Sketch Grammar of the Karlong Variety of Mongghul, and dialectal Survey of Mongghul* (unpublished doctoral dissertation, University of Hawaii, 2007).

Fried, Mary Heather Yazak, *Dressing Up, Dressing Down: Ethnic Identity Among the Tongren Tu of Northwest China* (unpublished doctoral dissertation, State University of New York, 2009).

Fried, Robert Wayne, *A Grammar of Bao'an Tu, A Mongolic Language or Northwest China* (unpublished doctoral dissertation, State University of New York, 2010).

Ha, Baocheng 哈宝成, *Hashi zuqun de lishi dianziban* 哈氏族群的历史电子版 [*Digital Version of the Ha Clan History*] (unpublished recording, 2010).

Ha, Mingzong, and C. K. Stuart, 'Everyday Hawan Mongghul', *Mongolica Pragensia*, 06 (2006), 45–70.

—, and C. K. Stuart, 'The return of the Goddess: Religious Revival among Hawan Village Mongghuls', *Mongolo-Tibetica Pragensia*, 1 (2) (2008), 117–148.

—, 'Politeness in Hawan Mongghul', *Mongolica Pragensia*, 07 (2007), 29–54.

—, Interview with Ha Shenglin, Hawan (Gansu, China, February 2005).

—, Interview with Ha Baode, Hawan (Gansu, China, September 2009).

—, Interview with Ha Zhanyuan, Xihajia (Qinghai, China, September 2009a).

—, Interview with Ha Shengcheng, Huazangsi (Gansu, China, September 2009b).

—, Interview with Gazangshiji and Wushisan, Dakeshidan (Gansu, China, September 2009c).

—, Interview with Ha Shenghui, Ha Shengcheng and Lan Deke, Hawan (Gansu, China, September 2009d).

—, 'Orální historie mongghulského rodu Ha' [Mongghul Ha Clan Oral History] (unpublished bachelor's thesis, Charles University Prague, 2010).

—, Interview with Ha Lianying, Akesu (Xinjiang, China, July 2010).

—, Interview with Ha Shengcai, Ha Shengzhang, and Ha Baoshan, Hawan (Gansu, China, August, 2011).

Ha, Shoude 哈守德 and Li Zhanzhong 李占忠, *Tianzhu tuzu* 天祝土族, (Tianzhu 天祝: Tianzhu zangzu zizhixian minzu chubanshe天祝藏族自治县民族出版社) [*Tianzhu Mongghul*, (Tianzhu: People's Press of Tianzhu Tibetan Autonomous County, 1999)].

Hu, Alex, 'An Overview of the History and Culture of the Xianbei ('Monguor'/'Tu')', *Asian Ethnicity*, 11 (1) (2010), 95–146.

Janhunen, Juha and Ha Mingzong et al., 'On the Language of the Shaowa Tuzu in the Context of the Ethnic Taxonomy of Amdo Qinghai', *Central Asiatic Journal*, 51 (2) (2007), 177–195.

Janhunen, Juha, ed., *The Mongolic Languages* (London and New York: Routledge, 2003).

—, 'The Monguor: The Emerging Diversity of a Vanishing People', in *The Monguors of the Kansu-Tibetan Frontier*, by Louis M. J. Schram, ed. by Charles Kevin Stuart (Xining City: Plateau Publications, 2006), pp. 26–29.

—, and M. Peltomaa et al., *Wutun* (München: Lincom Europa, 2008).

Li, Shenghua 李生华, 'Tuzu juefei tuyuhun houyi 土族绝非吐谷浑后裔' ['The Tu people are not Tuyuhun descendants'], *Qinghai Social Sciences*青海社会科学, 4 (2004), 149–160.

Li, Keyu李克郁, and Li, Meiling李美玲, *Hehuang menggu'er ren* 河湟蒙古尔人 (Xining 西宁: Qinghai renmin chubanshe青海人民出版社) [Hehuang Mongols (Xining: Qinghai People's Press, 2005)].

Li, Zhanzhong李占忠 and Wangxiang Yan 闫万象 et al., Gansu tuzu wenhua xingtai yu guji wencun 甘肃土族文化形态与古籍文存. *Gansu shaoshu minzu guji congshu* 甘肃少数民族古籍丛书 (Lanzhou兰州: Gansu minzu chubanshe甘肃民族出版社) [*Culture Configuration and Historical Records of Gansu Tu Nationality. Historical Records of Nationalities in Gansu* (Lanzhou: Gansu Nationalities Press, 2004)].

Limusishiden, (Li Dechun) and C K Stuart, 'Relevance to Current Monguor Ethnographic Research', in *The Monguors of the Kansu-Tibetan Frontier*, by Louis M. J. Schram, ed. by Charles Kevin Stuart (Xining City: Plateau Publications, 2006), pp. 60–79.

Lü, Jianfu 吕建福, *Tuzu shi* 土族史, (Beijing北京: Zhongguo shehui kexue chubanshe 中国社会科学出版社) [*Tu History* (Beijing: Chinese Social Sciences Press, 2002)].

Mostaert, Antoine and A. de Smedt, 'Le dialecte Monguor parlé par les Mongols du Kansu Occidental (I+II)', *Anthropos*, 24 (1929), 145–65, 801–815.

—, 'Le dialecte Monguor parlé par les Mongols du Kansu Occidental (III+IV)', *Anthropos*, 25 (1930), 657–69, 961–973.

—, 'Le dialecte Monguor parlé par les Mongols du Kansu Occidental (V)', *Anthropos*, 26 (1931), 253–254.

Nietupski, Paul, 'Louis Schram and the Study of Social and Political History', in *The Monguors of the Kansu-Tibetan Frontier*, by Louis M. J. Schram, ed. by Charles Kevin Stuart (Xining City: Plateau Publications, 2006), pp. 30–36.

Roche, Gerald and Ban+de mkhar et al., 'Participatory Culture Documentation on the Tibetan Plateau', in *Language Documentation and Description, Vol 8*, ed. by Imogen Gunn and Mark Turin (London: SOAS, 2010), pp. 147–165.

Sagaster, Klaus, 'The Mongols of Kansu and their Language', in *Antoine Mostaert, Vol. 2*, ed. by Klaus Sagaster (Ferdinant Verbiest Foundation: Leuven, 1999) pp. 175-190.

Schram, Louis M. J., *The Monguors of the Kansu-Tibetan Frontier, Part I: Their Origin, History, and Social Organization; Part II: Their Religious Life; Part III: Records of the Monguor Clans: History of the Monguors in Huangchung and the Chronicles of the*

Lu Family, ed. by Charles Kevin Stuart (Xining: Plateau Publications 2006 [1954, 1957, 1961]).

Schröder, Dominik, 'Zur Religion der Tujen des Sininggebietes (Kukunor)', *Anthropos*, 47 (1952), 1–79, 620–658, 822–870.

—, 'Zur Religion der Tujen des Sininggebietes (Kukunor)', *Anthropos*, 48 (1953), 202–259.

—, *Aus der Volksdichtung der Monguor* [From the Popular Poetry of the Monguor]; *1. Teil: Das weibe Glücksschaf (Mythen, Märchen, Lieder)* [Part 1. The White Lucky-Sheep (Myths, Fairytales, Songs)]. Asiatische Forschungen 6 (Wiesbaden: Otto Harrassowitz, 1959).

—, 'Der dialekt der Monguor', in *Mongolistik (Handbuch der Orientalistik, 1. Abteilung, 5. Band, 2. Abschnit)*, ed. by B. Spuler (Leiden: EJ Brill, 1964), pp. 143-158.

—, *Aus der Volksdichtung der Monguor* [From the Popular Poetry of the Monguor]; *2. Teil: In den Tagen der Urzeit (Ein Mythus vom Licht und vom Leben)* [Part 2. In the Days of Primeval Times (A Myth of Light and Life)] (Wiesbaden: Otto Harrassowitz, 1970).

Slater, Keith W., *A Grammar of Mangghuer: A Mongolic Language of China's Qinghai-Gansu Sprachbund* (New York: Routledge Curzon, 2003).

—, 'Mangghuer', in *The Mongolic Languages*, ed. by Juha Janhunen (London and New York: Routledge, 2003a), pp. 307–324.

Stuart, Charles Kevin, and Limusishiden (Li Dechun), 'China's Monguor Minority: Ethnography and Folktales', *Sino-Platonic Papers*, 59 (1994).

Online Sources

Ha Baocheng, *A Digital Version of Ha Clan History*
    <http://hbcdata.home.news.cn/blog/>

Website about Tu people
    <http://www.e56.com.cn/system_file/minority/tuzu/lishi.htm>

World Oral Literature Project, *Ha Mingzong: Mongghul Ha Clan Oral History*
    <http://www.oralliterature.org/collections/hmingzong001.html>

Index

≠Akhoe Hai//om 4, 6, 13
'Iipay 91
!Khwa ttu \
 San Culture & Education 83

Aboriginal (art/artists) 83
academia 77
academic xxii, 22, 23, 44, 59, 75, 76, 80,
 85, 95, 130, 135
access xiii, xv-xvii, xxii, xxiii, 9-12, 14-
 17, 21-23, 25-30, 32, 33, 36-38, 43, 47,
 94, 95, 99, 118, 119, 147
 control xvii, 24, 36
 management 9, 26
 protocol 28, 30, 31
 rights 9, 10, 12, 14, 16, 30
 system xvii, 26, 37
accessibility xvii, 33-35, 49, 99, 114, 117, 118
account xvii, xix-xxi, 26-28, 70, 111, 138, 147
Aduamah, E.Y. 67
Adzovia clan 67
Agbogbo 69
Aguigah 65, 67
Ahmed, Martha 49
Amazon 103, 105, 108
Amedzɔ fe 75
amega 68
Ameka, Felix xvii, xix, 66, 69, 76-78, 84
Amenumey, D.E.K. 65, 67, 75
ancestors 73, 78, 96, 133, 134, 136, 138-
 140, 145
Anlo 65-68, 70, 72, 76, 79
 stool 67
Anloga 66, 67, 70, 77, 79
annotation 34
anthropological discourse 49
applied linguists 22

Arabic 34, 68, 74
Arcadia Fund 3
archive(s) xvi, xvii, xviii, 3-9, 12, 13,
 18, 21, 22, 25-31, 35-37, 45-48, 55, 59,
 95, 99, 124, 127, 132 *See also* digital
 archive(s)
archiving xiv, xvi, xvii, xx, xxi, 3, 4,
 11, 14, 17, 18, 22, 23, 25, 37, 38, 44, 55,
 59, 94, 95, 110, 116, 126, 127, 130-132
 See also digital archiving
archiving software 6, 8, 12
Ashanti 72, 75
audience xviii, xix, xxii, 26, 47, 50, 70,
 73, 74, 77, 85, 116, 127, 131
audio xv, xx, 4, 8, 25, 30, 33, 34, 41, 44,
 46, 49, 53-56, 95, 125, 132, 146
 and video recordings xiv, 4, 7, 116, 145
 .-video documentation 145
Augé, M. 81, 85
authentic xxi, 130, 131
 authenticity 127
authority 46, 67, 68
authorship (collaborative) 82, 84-86
Awapit 103-105

Baja California xix, 91, 99
Bakhtin, Mikhail 45
Baocheng, Ha 138, 139
Bate clan 67
Benda-Beckmann, Keebet and Franz
 von 10
Benin 65, 67, 75, 79
blogs 36
browser 33, 36, 58
browsing 31-33
Buda, Hala 138
Buddhism 75

This book does not end here...

At Open Book Publishers, we are changing the nature of the traditional academic book. The title you have just read will not be left on a library shelf, but will be accessed online by hundreds of readers each month across the globe. We make all our books free to read online so that students, researchers and members of the public who can't afford a printed edition can still have access to the same ideas as you.

Our digital publishing model also allows us to produce online supplementary material, including extra chapters, reviews, links and other digital resources. Find *Oral Literature in the Digital Age* on our website to access its online extras. Please check this page regularly for ongoing updates, and join the conversation by leaving your own comments:

http://www.openbookpublishers.com/isbn/9781909254305

If you enjoyed this book, and feel that research like this should be available to all readers, regardless of their income, please think about donating to us. Our company is run entirely by academics, and our publishing decisions are based on intellectual merit and public value rather than on commercial viability. We do not operate for profit and all donations, as with all other revenue we generate, will be used to finance new Open Access publications. For further information about what we do, how to donate to OBP, additional digital material related to our titles or to order our books, please visit our website.

The World Oral Literature Project is an urgent global initiative to document and disseminate endangered oral literatures before they disappear without record. Our website houses collections of recordings of oral literature, free-to-download publications of documentation theory and practice, and links to resources and funding for oral tradition fieldwork and archiving:

www.oralliterature.org

In partnership with Open Book Publishers, the World Oral Literature Project has launched a book series on oral literature. The series preserves and promotes the oral literatures of indigenous people by publishing materials on endangered traditions in innovative ways.

OpenBook
Publishers

Knowledge is for sharing